Derivatives For The Trading Floor

Patrick Boyle and Jesse McDougall

ISBN: 8673108987
ISBN-13: 9798673108987

Chapters

Table of Contents

Chapter 1

WHAT ARE FINANCIAL DERIVATIVES?

A *financial derivative* is an economic contract whose value depends on or is derived from the value of another instrument or underlying asset. Derivatives are categorized by the relationship between the underlying asset (the "underlying") and the derivative such as a forward, option, or swap[1]); the type of underlying asset (such as equity derivatives, foreign exchange derivatives, interest rate derivatives, commodity derivatives, or credit derivatives); the market in which they trade (such as exchange-traded or over-the-counter); and their pay-off profiles.

Derivatives can be used for speculative purposes or to hedge. A speculator is a trader who is taking positions with the goal of making a profit. A hedger is a trader who already has an economic exposure who takes an offsetting position (a hedge) in order to reduce a risk they already have exposure to. Very commonly, companies buy currency forwards (agreements to make trade a currency exchanges at a future date) in order to limit (hedge against) losses due to fluctuations in the exchange rate of two currencies, this is an example of hedging. Third parties sometimes use publicly available derivative prices as educated predictions of

---

[1] See page 23 of 346 for the definitions of these three terms.

uncertain future outcomes, for example, the likelihood that a corporation will default on its debts.

How are Financial Derivatives Used?

Derivatives are used by investors for the following purposes:

- Hedging or mitigating risk in an underlying. By entering into a derivative contract whose value moves in the opposite direction to their underlying position, hedgers aim to reduce their risk.
- Speculate and make a profit if the value of the underlying asset moves the way they expect.
- Obtain exposure to an underlying where it is not possible to trade in the underlying (e.g., weather derivatives).
- Provide leverage, such that a small movement in the underlying value can cause a large difference in the value of the derivative.
- Define their risk—traders can use options to give them quite defined risk exposures, such as setting a maximum loss for a position.
- Tailored exposures—derivatives traders can take positions that profit if an underlying moves in a given direction, stays in or out of a specified range, or reaches a certain level.

What are Financial Derivatives Underlyings?

There are numerous underlyings for derivatives available right now, and new ones are being developed every year.

- Equities of companies listed on public exchanges, such as General Electric, Citigroup, or Vodaphone.
- Fixed income instruments, such as government bonds, corporate bonds, credit spreads, or baskets of mortgages.
- Commodities, such as gold, oil, silver, cotton, or electricity.

- Indices, such as the FTSE 100, Hang Seng of Hong Kong, or Nikkei of Japan.
- Foreign exchange.
- Weather, such as the average temperature at a defined location or the amount of rainfall.
- Events, such as football games or shipping catastrophes.

Who Uses Financial Derivatives?

Hedgers

Hedgers are often producers or consumers of an underlying. They can be companies that are required to typically have exposure to particular underlyings in the normal running of their businesses. Derivatives allow risk related to the price of the underlying asset to be transferred from one party to another. For example, a corn farmer and a cereal manufacturing company like Kellogg's could sign a futures contract to exchange a specified amount of cash for a specified amount of corn in the future. Both parties have reduced a future risk, and thus are hedgers. Both parties reduce their exposure to sudden variations in the price of corn which could materially affect their respective businesses.

Another example would be if a corporation borrows a large sum of money at a specific interest rate and that interest rate resets every six months. The corporation is concerned that the rate of interest may be much higher in six months. The corporation could buy a derivative called a forward rate agreement (FRA), which is a contract to pay a fixed rate of interest six months after purchase on a pre-agreed upon notional amount of money. If the interest rate after six months is above the contract rate, the seller will pay the difference to the corporation, or FRA buyer. If the rate is lower, the corporation will pay the difference to the seller. The purchase of the FRA serves to reduce the uncertainty concerning interest rates and stabilize earnings. This allows the company's management to make better long-term business plans.

Speculators

Speculators are usually individuals who seek exposure to risky assets with the aim of making a profit. They are often pension plan managers, insurance companies, or asset management companies. Financial speculation can involve trading (buying, holding, selling) and short-selling of stocks, bonds, commodities, currencies, collectibles, real estate, derivatives, or *any* valuable asset to attempt to profit from fluctuations in its price irrespective of its underlying value. Many texts attempt to differentiate the concept of speculation from investing, but for this text a speculator and investor are the same thing. They are individuals or companies who take a derivatives position with the goal of profiting from it, rather than with the goal of reducing their risk or hedging their exposure. In the derivatives markets, the ratio of hedgers to speculators is constantly changing and will vary significantly based upon the type of derivative and type of underlying. In most markets however, speculators are both more numerous and trade higher volumes than hedgers.

Arbitrageurs

Arbitrage is the practice of taking advantage of a price difference between two or more markets. It usually involves the simultaneous purchase and sale of an asset, the profit being the difference between the market prices. It is a trade that profits by exploiting price differences of identical or similar financial instruments, on different markets or in different forms. Arbitrage exists as a result of market inefficiencies; it provides a mechanism to ensure prices do not deviate substantially from fair value for long periods of time. When used by academics, an arbitrage is a transaction that involves no probability of a negative cash flow at any point in time and a positive cash flow in at least one state—in simple terms, it has the *possibility* of a risk-free profit at zero cost. In industry the term arbitrage is more loosely used, often by marketers to describe trading strategies that in no way meet these standards. For the purposes of this book we will be using the academic definition, as this concept is extremely important as you will see later as a theoretical underpinning of almost all of our derivatives pricing methods.

Arbitrage is possible when one of three conditions is met:

1. The same asset does not trade at the same price on all markets ("which would be contra to the law of one price").
2. Two assets with identical cash flows and identical risk do not trade at the same price.
3. An asset with a known price in the future does not today trade at its future price discounted at the risk-free interest rate (or, the asset does not have negligible costs of storage—for example, this condition holds for commodities but not for securities).

Arbitrage is not simply the act of buying a product in one market and selling it in another for a higher price at some later time. To be considered a genuine "arbitrage," the offsetting transactions must occur simultaneously to avoid exposure to market risk, or the risk that prices may change on one market before both transactions are complete. In practical terms, this is generally possible only with securities and financial products that can be traded electronically. Even then, as each leg of the trade is executed, the prices in one of the venues may have moved. Missing one of the legs of the trade, and subsequently having to trade it soon after at a different price, is called "execution risk" or "legging risk." In practice, true arbitrages, risk-less, costless profitable opportunities, almost never occur, and any trading strategies that uses the term "arbitrage" is referring to near-arbitrage, or quasi-arbitrage situations, where the risk of financial loss is ultimately borne by the traders.

Middlemen
Middlemen are usually investment banks, market makers or brokers. They trade derivatives with the goal of earning either a commission or the bid-ask spread between customers undertaking opposing positions. A broker is an individual or brokerage firm that arranges transactions between buyers and sellers, and gets a commission when the deal is executed. A market maker is a company, or an individual, that quotes both a buy and a sell price

in a financial instrument or commodity held in inventory, hoping to make a profit on the difference—the bid-ask spread. These market participants typically are not aiming to accurately predict or profit from movements in the price of the underlying, they just aim to profit from the commission or spread. While in the ordinary running of their businesses they can end up holding a position which causes a profit or loss, they typically aim to avoid this and will usually hedge any residual exposures they are left with, if possible. Middlemen benefit from churn, a high volume of activity, in markets rather than from accurate directional positioning of their portfolios.

How are Derivatives Traded?

There are two groups of derivative contracts, which are distinguished by the way they are traded in the market: Over-the-counter derivatives and exchange-traded derivatives.

Over-the-counter derivatives (OTC)

Over-the-counter derivatives are contracts that are traded directly between two parties, without going through an exchange. Products such as swaps, forward rate agreements, exotic options—and other exotic derivatives—are typically traded in this way. The OTC derivatives market is the largest market for derivatives. The OTC market is largely made up of banks, large corporations, and other highly sophisticated parties. Knowing the size of the OTC market is not easy as trades can occur in private, without the activity being visible on any exchange. According to the Bank for International Settlements, the total outstanding notional amount of OTC derivatives is US$532 trillion as of June 2017. Of this total notional amount, approximately 67% are interest rate contracts, 8% are credit default swaps (CDS), 9% are foreign exchange contracts, 2% are commodity contracts, 1% are equity contracts, and 12% are classified as "other." Because OTC derivatives are not traded on an exchange, there is no central counter-party. Thus they are subject to counter-party risk, the risk of one party defaulting at settlement or closure of the contract, like any ordinary legal contract. Despite the complexity risks of OTC trading, most transactions are quite standardized, with standardized documentation.

There is a large push from governments and financial regulators, post-2008, to bring a sizeable proportion of the OTC markets onto "clearing" platforms. Controllable, transparent, and measurable market flows with clearinghouses providing trade completion assurance to all counterparties adds to overall financial stability.

Exchange-traded derivatives
Exchange-traded derivatives are those that are traded via a specialized derivatives exchange such as the CME group or Eurex Exchange. A derivatives exchange is a market where standardized contracts that have been defined by the exchange are traded. A derivatives exchange acts as an intermediary to all related transactions, and takes margin payments from the customers who trade with them to act as a guarantee. According to the Bank for International Settlements, the combined turnover in the world's derivatives exchanges totaled $8,989 billion in June 2018. Some types of derivative instruments also may trade on traditional exchanges. For instance, hybrid instruments such as convertible bonds and/or convertible preferred stock may be listed on stock or bond exchanges. Warrants or rights may be listed on equity exchanges (see Chapter 3).

Most exchange traded derivatives are traded electronically. Historically, financial markets were physical locations where buyers and sellers met and negotiated. With the improvement in communications technology in the late 20th century, the need for a physical location became less important, since traders could transact from remote locations. One of the earliest examples of widespread electronic trading was on Globex, the CME Group's electronic trading platform that allows access to a variety of financial, foreign exchange, and commodity markets. The Chicago Board of Trade produced a rival system "E Open Outcry," an electronic trading platform that allowed for electronic trading to take place alongside the trading that took place in the CBOT pits. Electronic trading makes transactions easier to complete, monitor, clear, and settle. Electronic trading brought down the cost of trading, improved liquidity and increased transparency when introduced.

What are the Most Popular Types of Derivatives?

The best known types of derivative contracts are as follows:

1. **Forwards**: An OTC contract between two parties, where payment takes place at a specific time in the future at today's predetermined price.
2. **Futures**: An exchange-listed contract to buy or sell an asset on or before a future date at a price specified today. A futures contract differs from a forward contract in that the futures contract is a standardized contract which is then backed by a clearing house working with an exchange where the contract can be bought and sold; the forward contract is a non-standardized OTC contract written by the parties themselves.
3. **Options**: An option is a derivative financial instrument that specifies a contract between two parties for a future transaction on an asset at a reference price—the strike. The buyer of the option gains the right, but not the obligation, to engage in that transaction, while the seller incurs the corresponding obligation to fulfil the transaction. Options can be either exchange-traded or OTC. An option which conveys the right to buy something at a specific price is called a *call*; an option which conveys the right to sell something at a specific price is called a *put*.
4. **Warrants**: A warrant is quite similar to an option, but it is typically issued by a company on its own stock and, when exercised, new equity is issued causing ownership dilution to common stock holders.
5. **Swaps**: A swap is an OTC derivative in which counterparties exchange *cash flows* of one party's financial instrument for those of the other party's financial instrument.

What is the Economic Function of Derivatives Markets?

Some of the key economic functions of the derivatives market include:

1. The derivatives market reallocates risk from the risk averse to those willing to take risk with the expectation of a reasonable return. This ability to spread risk stimulates the economy as otherwise businesses might stop trading once they had reached a threshold of risk beyond which they were unwilling to go.
2. The derivatives markets allow participants to hedge and manage their existing economic exposures.
3. Derivatives are essential tools to determine both current prices and a best estimate of future prices.
4. Derivatives can improve market efficiency for the underlying asset. Investors can buy an S&P500 future and have much lower trading costs than if they were to buy all 500 stocks individually.

What are the Criticisms of Derivatives Markets?

1. Derivatives can give hedgers a false sense of security. Investors may calculate the correlations between various market instruments and believe they are hedged. Yet in extreme events as in the default on Russian government debt in 1998, correlations between two assets (that, in combination, are expected to reduce overall volatility in a portfolio) that are zero or negative in normal times can turn overnight to be highly correlated. A phenomenon that academics have referred to as "phase lock-in." A hedged position can become unhedged at the worst times, inflicting substantial losses on those who mistakenly believe they are protected.

2. The use of derivatives can result in large losses because of the use of *leverage*. Derivatives allow investors to earn large returns from small movements in the underlying asset's price. However, investors could lose considerable amounts if the price of the underlying moves against them significantly.
3. The size and complexity of the derivatives markets can bring about market contagion, such as was seen in the financial crisis after the failure of Lehman Brothers in 2008.

Are Financial Derivatives a Zero Sum Game?

In game theory and economic theory, a zero-sum game is a mathematical representation of a situation in which a participant's gain (or loss) of utility is exactly balanced by the losses (or gains) of the utility of the other participant(s). If the total gains of the participants are added up, and the total losses are subtracted, they will sum to zero. Many economic situations are not zero-sum, since valuable goods and services can be created, destroyed, or allocated in a number of ways, and any of these will create a net gain or loss of utility to the combined various stakeholders.

Derivatives are bilateral contracts, so one party's loss is equal to its counterparty's gain and therefore the transaction as a whole is a zero-sum game. Often derivatives traders also trade in the underlying security, such as trading a stock option against the underlying stock. In this case their overall outcome will not be a zero sum game due to the impact of the underlying security.

Certain securities, such as mortgage-backed bonds, can be considered derivatives, but the line between securities and derivatives is quite easy to understand. Derivatives are a zero-sum game, while if a security goes to zero, no one else makes a corresponding profit.

Chapter 1 Questions

1. What is the difference between a hedger and a speculator?

2. If an arbitrage opportunity were to appear in a market, how would you expect traders to react? Over time, how persistent would you expect the opportunity to remain and why?

3. Is it reasonable to expect financial markets to be arbitrage free?

4. Is a futures contract a form of forward contract? Discuss your answer.

5. Does the existence of derivatives increase the overall riskiness of markets? Discuss.

6. Define a financial derivative.

7. How might options be used by investors to define their risk compared to a position in a single stock?

8. What is the role of a middleman in the derivatives market? How do they make money?

9. How do over-the-counter derivatives differ from exchange-traded derivatives?

10. How does a warrant differ from an option?

11. Explain the term "zero sum game." Are derivatives a zero sum game?

12. What is a swap contract?

13. Explain how the existence of a derivatives market could benefit individuals in society who never trade derivatives?

14. At times of volatility in the equities and commodities markets, politicians and public commentators have argued that

speculation in futures is purely gambling. Discuss aspects of social utility provided by allowing speculators to trade futures.

15. What happens if an exchange introduces a new futures contract where the quality of the underlying asset was imperfectly specified?

Chapter 2

WHAT ARE FUTURES & FORWARDS?

Financial Futures

A *futures contract* is a standardized financial contract obligating the buyer to purchase an asset, and the seller to sell an asset, at a predetermined future date and price. Futures contracts specify in detail the quality and quantity of the underlying asset. The contracts are standardized to facilitate trading on a futures exchange. Some futures contracts may call for physical delivery of the asset, while others are settled in cash.

The price at which the transaction will take place is known as the futures price or strike price. The delivery and payment occur at a specified future date known as the delivery date. The contracts are negotiated at a futures exchange, which acts as an intermediary between the two parties. The party agreeing to buy the underlying asset in the future, the "buyer" of the contract, is said to be "long," and the party agreeing to sell the asset in the future, the "seller" of the contract, is said to be "short."

The History of Futures Markets

Aristotle described the story of Thales of Miletus, a poor philosopher who used his skill in forecasting and predicted that the olive harvest would be exceptionally good the next autumn. Thales made agreements with local olive press owners to deposit his money with them to guarantee him exclusive use of their olive presses when the harvest was ready. Thales successfully negotiated low prices because the harvest was in the future and no one knew whether the harvest would be plentiful or poor and because the olive press owners were willing to hedge against the possibility of a poor yield. When the harvest time came, and the harvest was good, many presses were wanted concurrently and Thales provided access to presses at very high rental rates, and made a large quantity of money.

The first futures exchange market was the Dōjima Rice Exchange in Japan in the 1730s, which was built to meet the needs of samurai who, being paid in rice, after a series of bad harvests needed a stable conversion to coin.

The Chicago Board of Trade (CBOT) listed the first ever standardized "exchange traded" forward contracts in 1864, which were called futures contracts. These contracts were based on grain and started a trend that saw contracts created on a number of different commodities, as well as a number of futures exchanges set up in countries around the world.

Standardization in Financial Futures Markets

Futures contracts are highly standardized. They usually specify:

1. The underlying asset or instrument. This could be anything from commodities to currencies to financial securities.
2. The type of settlement, either cash settlement or physical settlement.
3. The amount and units of the underlying asset per contract.

4. The currency in which the futures contract is quoted.
5. The grade of the deliverable. This is usually extremely specific. For example a wheat futures contract will specify the variety of wheat, its quality, and even the protein content.
6. The last trading time and date and the delivery date and location.
7. Details such as the tick size, which is the minimum permissible price fluctuation.

What is Futures Margin?

The term *margin* refers to borrowed money that is used to purchase securities. Buying securities in a leveraged manner is referred to as "buying on margin." The amount of margin posted, the *collateral,* refers to the amount of equity contributed by a customer as a percentage of the current market value of the securities. The reason that exchanges and counterparties demand margin is to minimize credit risk. Typically, traders must post margin or a liquid bond, sometimes called a performance bond, of between 5% and 15% of the contract's value. Futures margin rates are set by the futures exchanges. Some brokerages will add an extra premium to the exchange minimum rate in order to lower their risk exposure to a particular client. Margin is usually set based on risk. The larger the typical dollar value movements in an asset class , the higher the margin rates will be for futures contracts that are based upon that asset.

To minimize counterparty risk to traders, trades executed on regulated futures exchanges are guaranteed by a clearing house. The clearing house is a separate entity from the market participants buying and selling the assets, and separate from the middlemen or market-makers, set up solely to enhance market participants' assurance against failure to pay on behalf of losing counterparties. Clearing houses become the counterparty to each seller and buyer in the instruments they clear. A clearing house stands between two member firms and its purpose is to reduce the risk of any firm failing to honor its trade settlement obligations. A clearing house reduces the settlement risks by:

1. Netting offsetting transactions between multiple counterparties
2. Requiring collateral margin deposits
3. Providing independent valuation of trades and collateral
4. Monitoring the creditworthiness of the firms which clear through them
5. Providing a guarantee fund that can be used to cover losses that exceed a defaulting member firm's collateral on deposit.

Margin requirements enable traders to transact without performing due diligence on each counterparty they deal with, thus facilitating an orderly market with greatly enhanced liquidity. Margin requirements are reduced in many cases for hedgers who have physical ownership of the covered commodity, in effect, collateral, or spread traders who have offsetting contracts balancing the position.

Initial Futures Margin is the amount of money that is required to initiate a buy or sell position on a futures contract. Initial margin requirement is calculated based on the maximum estimated change in contract value within a trading day and is set by the exchange.

Margin Maintenance is the set minimum margin per outstanding futures contract that a customer must maintain in their margin account. For example, suppose the margin on an oil futures contract is $100 and the maintenance margin is $70. If you buy ten oil futures contracts you will need to have $1,000 set aside for the initial margin. If the price of oil drops such that you lose $300 or more, you have violated the maintenance level and need to add funds to bring it back to the initial maintenance level.

Margin Calls a margin call on futures contracts is triggered when the value of your account drops below the maintenance level and it entails the broker asking its client, hedger or speculator, to deposit sufficient funds into their account to maintain their trading position, including all maintenance margin required. If the cash margins held against futures contracts are insufficient, brokers close out losing positions on traders.

Financial Forwards

A *forward contract* is a non-standardized contract between two parties to buy or sell an asset at a specified future time at a price agreed upon today. The party agreeing to buy the underlying asset in the future assumes a long position, and the party agreeing to sell the asset in the future assumes a short position. The price agreed upon is called the *delivery price*, which is equal to the forward price at the time the contract is entered into. Forwards are substantially similar to futures, with these important differences:

1. Forwards are private contracts and do not trade on organized exchanges. Futures contracts trade on organized exchanges.
2. Forwards are customized contracts satisfying the needs of the parties involved. Futures contracts are highly standardized.
3. Forwards are contracts with the originating counterparty; a single clearing house is the counterparty to all futures contracts, forwards need not be associated with any clearing house.
4. Forward contracts are usually not regulated. The government regulates the futures markets.
5. Forwards typically have no interim partial settlements or "margin requirements" like futures. However, being traded over-the-counter (OTC), forward contract specification can be customized and may include mark-to-market[2] and daily

---

[2] Mark-to-market refers to the process of measuring the profits and losses of a position or portfolio of assets at a given point in time (frequently performed at daily close of business) to generate as accurate of a valuation as possible of a financial situation. Each item in a portfolio, in this process, will be marked

margining such that if the value of the forward drops below a threshold then additional margin may be required.

The Fair Value of a Futures Contract

When the underlying asset exists in plentiful supply then the price of a futures contract is determined via no-arbitrage arguments[3]. This is the case for stock index futures, treasury bond futures, and futures on physical commodities when they are in supply such as agricultural crops after the harvest. When the underlying is not in plentiful supply or when it does not yet exist—for example, on crops before the harvest or on Eurodollar futures in which the underlying instrument is to be created upon the delivery date—the futures price cannot be fixed by arbitrage. In this scenario the price is fixed by supply and demand for the asset in the future, which is supply and demand for the futures contract.

Notation: In this book we will be using the following notation for formulas:

T = Time to delivery, denoted in years
S_0 = Spot price of the underlying today, at time zero, at trade inception
F_0 = Forward/futures price today
r = Risk free rate annualized
f = Value of the futures contract today

In the example of an underlying asset that is in plentiful supply, such as S&P500 futures, an arbitrage argument can be made that the futures price represents the expected future value of the underlying

---

(valued) to its current liquidation value based on live market prices where available.

[3] The no-arbitrage argument in securities valuation is that if there are two portfolios with identical payoffs they must have the same valuation at a given point in time. This helps to price derivatives based on portfolios which contain varying proportions of an underlying, a derivative on that underlying, and a risk-free asset. Further examples of this are outlined in Chapter 6 and in Chapter 17.

discounted at the risk-free rate (the rate of return on a risk free investment. Any deviation from the theoretical price would offer investors a riskless profit opportunity -- it would attract buyers of the underpriced asset and sellers of the overpriced asset, driving the relationship between the prices back to its arbitrage-free state. . Thus, the price for such a futures contract will be determined by the following formula:

$$F_0 = S_0 \times e^{rT}$$

Here is an example of how arbitrage helps us to determine the futures/forward price. Suppose we have no idea what futures price we should agree on for a futures contract. We know a share's price right now is $40. Suppose futures are available in the market for you to sell at $43 with a 3 month maturity. Interest rates are at 5%. How do we know if this is fair value or not?

The share costs $40 now. We could borrow $40 at r = 5% for 3 months and use these funds to buy 1 share. We could then sell a Futures contract on 1 share. At expiration, regardless of what has happened to the share price between now and maturity, we would hand over the 1 share to our counterparty, receive $43 and owe back $40 × $e^{0.05 \times 3/12}$=$40.50. This transaction would earn us $43 − $40.50 = $2.50 per contract. In such a scenario we should make this trade as big as we can. The counterparty's losses would be equal to our profits, and they would have to adjust their futures price quickly to fair value in order to avoid bankruptcy.

In a perfect market, the relationship between futures and spot prices depends on the above formula. In the real world, there are various issues such as transaction costs, differential borrowing and lending rates, restrictions on short selling, and so on, that prevent complete arbitrage. Thus, the futures price in fact varies within arbitrage boundaries around the theoretical price.

This pricing relationship can be modified to take storage costs, dividends, or foreign currencies into account as follows:

Where q is the percentage dividend yield on a stock index, the formula is

$$F_0 = S_0 \times e^{(r-q)T}$$

If u is the percentage storage costs on an underlying, the formula is

$$F_0 = S_0 \times e^{(r+u)T}$$

When calculating the futures price of currency futures, S_0 is the spot exchange rate of the domestic currency with a risk free rate denoted as r. The foreign currency risk free rate is denoted as r_f, the formula for the currency futures contract valuation is (where S_0 is the exchange rate with domestic/foreign):

$$F_0 = S_0 \times e^{(r-rf)T}$$

What is Convenience Yield?

Users of a consumption asset may obtain a benefit from *physically* holding the asset which is not obtained from holding a futures contract. The classical example of this is heating oil in the winter. Market participants may happily pay more for physical heating oil than the future, simply because they need to use it to heat their homes, or run their businesses. This benefit is known as *convenience yield*. Everyone who owns inventory has the choice between consumption today versus investment for the future. A rational investor will choose the outcome that is best for them, based on whether or not it is important to them to have access to the consumption asset prior to a contract expiry.

The futures or forward contract price for an underlying asset with a convenience yield is: :

$$F_0 = S_0 \times e^{(r+u-y)T}$$

where y is the symbol for convenience yield.

It is important to understand that y is backed out of market prices. You can never be given a number in real life and told that it is the convenience yield for an asset. You reverse it out of market prices to understand what convenience yield is implying for the asset in question.

Futures Prices Converge to the Spot Price

As implied by the above formulas, the closer we get to a futures expiration date, futures prices converge toward the spot price (see Figure 2.1). The difference between the spot price and the futures price is known as the "basis" . There will usually be a different basis for each delivery month for each underlying. Usually basis is defined as spot price minus futures price, however, sometimes futures price minus spot price is used, and this usage depends on market conventions around whether or not assets typically trade at a premium to their associated futures contracts, or a discount, but would generally be understood by users of the contracts in question.

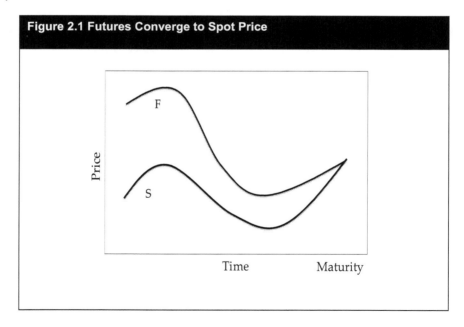

Figure 2.1 Futures Converge to Spot Price

The value of a futures contract at inception is always 0. It is important to clarify that here we are talking about value, rather than price. The value *f* of a futures contract midstream through its life is calculated using the following formula.

$$f = S_0 - Ke^{(-rT)}$$

Adhering to the usual definition, if the basis for each contract is positive and increasing with tenure, the market is in *backwardation*. If the basis for each contract is negative and decreasing with tenure (increasing in absolute value) then the market is in *contango*.

What are Backwardation and Contango?

The economist John Maynard Keynes argued that, in general, the natural hedgers of a commodity are those who wish to sell the commodity in the future. Thus, hedgers collectively hold a net short position in the forward market. The other side of these contracts must then be held by speculators, who must therefore hold a net long position. Hedgers are interested in reducing risk, and thus will accept losing money on their forward contracts. He argued that if speculators are holding a net long position, it must be the case that the expected future spot price is greater than the forward price.

This market situation, where the futures price is less than the expected spot price, is referred to as *normal backwardation*. Since the forward/futures prices converge with the spot price at maturity, normal backwardation implies that futures prices for a certain maturity are increasing over time.

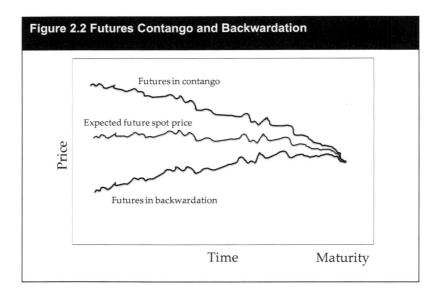

Figure 2.2 Futures Contango and Backwardation

Contango is a condition in which the distant delivery prices for futures exceeds spot prices. This is often due to the costs of storing and insuring the underlying commodity. Contango implies that futures prices for a certain maturity are falling over time. See Figure 2.2 for a graph depicting futures in contango or backwardation versus the expected future spot price of the underlying.

Why Hedge?

Most companies produce goods or provide services and may not have particular skills in predicting market prices such as interest rates, exchange rates, or commodity prices. If these are important drivers of a company's costs, often it makes sense to hedge these exposures and reduce business uncertainty, so that the company can focus on being the best they can be at their core expertise of providing goods or services.

- Short futures hedges are used when the company owns the asset already and expects to sell it in the future. Examples are farmers, gold mining companies, and petroleum producers.

- Long futures hedges are used when company knows it will have to purchase the asset in future. Examples are a breakfast cereal manufacturer needing to purchase grains or an airline company needing to purchase jet fuel to operate its fleet of planes.

Many people do not at first fully understand the concept of having exposure to a market variable. For example, let's look at an American company that manufactures goods. It buys all of its supplies locally in US dollars. It sells all of its goods to American consumers in US dollars, and pays its staff in US dollars. Does this company have any foreign exchange risk? Most people will answer no to this question, but if the company has one foreign competitor, they actually *are* exposed to foreign exchange rate risk. Should the price of the foreign currency fall in relation to the dollar, the foreign competitor has a cost advantage, and can undercut the US company's prices, potentially taking business from them.

Hedging Using Futures

Many users of futures are hedgers, but perfect hedges do not always exist in the futures market. A wheat farmer delivering crops having previously sold forward production using futures may experience a mismatch in timing, a mismatch in the precise quality of grain, or a mismatch in production size. Often a hedger has to hedge with an imperfect futures contract—something that is "close enough."

Cross hedging is offsetting a given economic exposure with a slightly different (but not entirely equivalent) asset. It is an imperfect hedge. For example, a farmer who raises an unusual strain of wheat may hedge with a more standard variety which has liquid futures contracts available on exchange.

A useful tool in helping to calculate the relationship between two assets to hedge optimally is the *minimum variance hedge ratio*, h. When your asset falls by 2% in a day, you want to be reasonably confident your hedge will rise 2% in the face of the same market dynamics.

Where ρ is the correlation between your exposure to a particular asset and the asset you are using to hedge and σ is the standard deviation of each asset.

$$h = \frac{\rho \cdot \sigma_{(exposure)}}{\sigma_{(futures)}}$$

Beta is a term used in markets to refer to the way in which an asset's price varies relative to the fluctuations of the overall market. "High beta" assets or stocks (those with a beta above 1) are those which tend to be highly correlated to the overall markets but with more volatility. "Low beta" assets or stocks (those with a beta below 1 or closer to zero) tend to be less correlated to overall markets and or have lower volatility. (Negative beta assets exist, but are more rare, and exhibit uncorrelated behaviour in their price movements as compared to overall markets.)

Beta is calculated as: β = (cov(portfolio, market)) / variance of the market. Variance of the market is the standard deviation of the market price returns squared.

You can hedge out the "market exposure" of a stock portfolio using overall market futures, which are assumed to have a beta β of 1 (see Chapter 10) with the following formula:

$$N = \frac{\beta \cdot V_A}{V_F}$$ where

V_A = value of stock portfolio

V_F = value of one futures contract

N = number of futures required to hedge

Does Hedging Make Sense?

Many academics and investors argue that shareholders can hedge themselves individually if they want to against certain market exposures and that therefore the companies they invest in should not hedge at all. Investors may for example have invested in a gold mining company because they felt that the price of gold was likely to rise. They may therefore be unhappy to find out that the mining company was hedging its exposure to gold, and thus if the price of gold was to rise, the investor would not experience the gains they were hoping for.

This is a good argument, and it is reasonable to say that an investor can be protected from excess exposures to certain economic variables either through holding a diversified portfolio, or through hedging the exposures on their own. This ignores the fact that hedges are cheaper if done in "size," that is, at the company level, rather than individually by each retail investor. The real argument, however, for a company doing at least some hedging is that it allows them to have some clarity of future prices, and this allows them to make more long-term business plans. For example, a breakfast cereal company might decide on the pricing of a box of oatmeal one year in advance. They might design a box with a price printed on it well into the future. If they are unable to hedge their short-term exposure to the price of oats, things may become quite difficult when negotiating pricing with supermarkets since their customers would find it annoying to find the price fluctuating every time they go shopping. The company may also have difficulty making any sort of long-term plans when their profit margins are unknown.

Order Types Used by Traders.

1. **Market Order:** An order to a broker to sell or buy at the prevailing market price.

2. **Limit Order:** An order to buy at no more than a specific price or to sell at no less than a specific price. Limit orders are used when the trader wishes to control price rather than certainty of execution. This gives the trader control over the price at which the trade is executed; however, the order may never be executed.

3. **Stop order or stop-loss:** An order to buy or sell once the price reaches a specified level, known as the stop price. When the stop price is reached, a stop order becomes a market order. A buy stop order is entered at a stop price above the current market price. A sell stop order is entered at a stop price below the current market price. Investors generally use a buy stop order to limit a loss or to protect a profit on something that they have sold short. Investors generally use a sell stop order to limit a loss or to protect a profit on something that they own. Certain exchanges have stopped offering stop order types. Beginning February 26, 2016, the New York Stock Exchange (NYSE) plans to no longer accept stop orders and good-till-canceled orders. The reason they gave was that "many retail investors use stop orders as a potential method of protection but don't fully understand the risk profile associated with the order type. We expect our elimination of stop orders will help raise awareness around the potential risks during volatile trading." Brokerage firms may still offer these order types to their customers, and execute them through in-house algorithms, but the orders will no longer be available directly from the exchange.

4. **Stop-limit:** An order that combines the features of a stop order and a limit order. Once the stop price is reached, the stop-limit order becomes a limit order to buy (or to sell) at no more (or less) than another, pre-specified limit price. As with all limit orders, a stop-limit order doesn't get filled if the security's price never reaches the specified limit price.

5. **Market-if-touched:** An order to trade at the best available price, if the market price first goes to the "if touched" level.

As soon as this trigger price is touched, the order becomes a market order.

6. **Discretionary or market-not-held order:** An order that uses the broker's discretion to try to get a better price.

Drawing Payoff Diagrams

Payoff diagrams for futures and forwards are simple because they are linear products. Much like being long or short the underlying, when you are long or short a future or forward, the price moving in your favor will generate a profit, and the price moving against you will generate a loss. The amount of profit or loss relates directly to how much the price has moved. The main reason we look at payoff diagrams at this point is so that students new to derivatives can understand payoff diagrams, which will make the more complex derivatives diagrams we get to later easy to understand.

First we look at diagrams that are long or short the underlying asset. These payoff profiles are shown in Figures 2.3 and 2.4.

In a long position, as the asset price moves up beyond your entry investment price, your profit increases As the asset price falls your losses increase in a linear manner. With the short position, as the price rises beyond your entry price you lose money and as the price falls you make money, all in a linear fashion.

Figure 2.3 shows the long position. Profits are unlimited, the asset price can, in theory, rises forever, but losses are capped to 100% of your investment. With a short position, Figure 2.4, gains are capped, as the asset cannot fall more than 100%, and losses are unlimited.

As you can see in Figures 2.5 and 2.6, the payoff profiles are identical for futures or forwards with the investor's entry price being the futures prices when they enter into their derivatives contracts and the ultimate payoff depends on the final futures price at expiration or close-out of the investor's position.

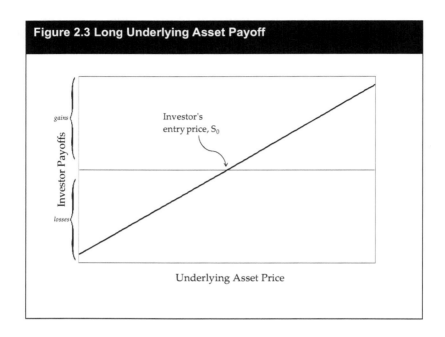

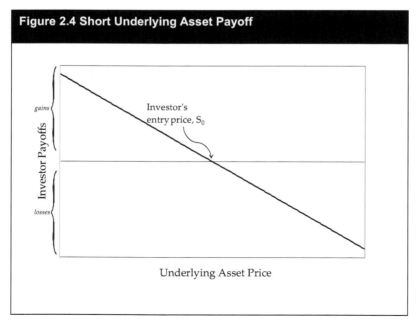

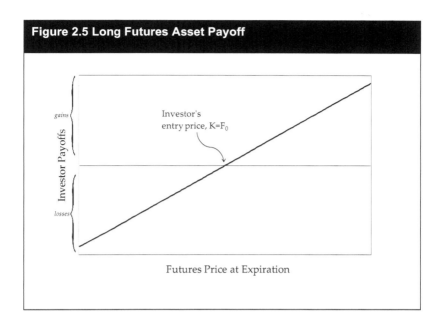

Figure 2.5 Long Futures Asset Payoff

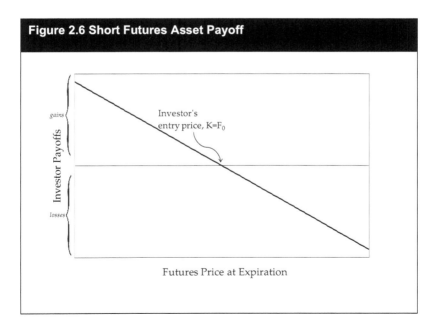

Figure 2.6 Short Futures Asset Payoff

Chapter 2 Questions

1. Describe how you think market participants would react if an exchange started trading a new contract in which the quality of the underlying asset was incompletely specified?

2. Why does settlement price matter for futures?

3. Explain why the futures price converges to the spot price? What would happen if this did not occur?

4. Is physical delivery necessary to ensure that futures prices converge to the spot price?

5. Why do futures traders have to post margin?

6. Is margin typically higher for speculators or hedgers? Why?

7. Explain what margin maintenance is.

8. How do dividends affect futures prices?

9. How do storage costs affect futures prices?

10. Explain backwardation and contango.

11. Explain the pros and cons of a company participating in hedging.

12. Some traders in the market operate as "day traders" or "scalpers" who trade to profit from tiny swings in futures prices, explain if and how this behavior benefits others?

13. How does a stop-limit order work? How does it differ from a stop-loss order? Why might a trader wish to use these order types?

14. In a market free from transaction costs, arbitrage opportunities, taxes, or restrictions from short selling, what would the fair price

be for an oil futures contract if spot oil is trading at $50, the risk-free rate is 5% (compounded semi-annually), and expiration is six months away?

15. Working from the information in the last question, if restrictions on short selling meant that a reverse cash-and-carry trader (one who is long the futures contract and simultaneously short the underlying asset) could only receive the use of 85% of the proceeds of oil sold short, what is the permissible range of oil futures prices?

16. Taking all of the information in the last two questions into account, if borrowing cost was 5%, but the lending rate was 4.5% (both compounded semi-annually), what now would be the permissible range of oil futures prices?

17. Explain why futures and forward prices might differ.

18. You manage a stock portfolio worth $100 million. The portfolio has a beta of 1.1. Explain how you would fully hedge this portfolio if the S&P500 futures contract is currently trading at 2000.

19. If you know the formula for correlation to be
$$\rho = \frac{cov(portfolio, market)}{\sigma_p \, \sigma_m}$$
, show that the minimum variance hedge ratio h when trying to "cross asset hedge" is equivalent to beta.

20. An auto manufacturing executive argues that there is no point to the company using metals futures. There is an equal chance that the price of input metals in the future will be less than the futures price as there is that they will be greater than this price. Discuss the pros and cons of the executive's opinion.

21. Options and futures are zero-sum games. Describe what is meant by this statement.

Chapter 3

WHAT ARE FINANCIAL OPTIONS?

Options Contracts

A financial *option* is a financial derivative instrument that specifies a contract between two parties for a future transaction on an asset at a reference price. The buyer of the option gains the right, but not the obligation, to engage in that transaction, while the seller incurs the corresponding obligation to fulfill the transaction. Options cost money to buy at inception while futures cost nothing to enter into, either as a buyer or as a seller, at inception.

There are two basic types of option: calls and puts.

What is in an Options Contract?

Each financial option is a legal contract between two counterparties with the terms of the option specified in a term sheet. Some exotic options may have extremely complicated term sheets, but all options contracts must contain the following specifications:

- A description of what the underlying asset is

- Whether the option holder has the right to buy or the right to sell the underlying
- The quantity and quality, or class, of the underlying asset
- The "strike price," which is the price at which the transaction will occur upon exercise
- The expiration date, which is the last date the option can be exercised
- Whether the writer must deliver the actual asset on exercise, or may simply tender the equivalent cash amount

Call Option Definition

The buyer of a *call option* has the right, but not the obligation, to buy an agreed lots of 100 shares of the option by the expiration, for a certain price: the strike price. The seller (or "writer") is obligated to sell the commodity or financial instrument should the buyer so decide.

The buyer pays a fee, called a *premium*, for this right.

Put Option Definition

The buyer of a *put option* has the right, but not an obligation, to sell lots of 100 shares of the asset at the strike price by the expiration date. The seller of the put option (or "writer") has the obligation to buy the asset at the strike price if the buyer exercises the option.

- The buyer pays a fee, called a premium, for this right.

For every buyer of an option, there must be a seller. The seller of an option is also sometimes called the writer of the option. There are four possible simple options positions, outlined in Figure 3.1.

Long call: The buyer of a call option has the right to buy an underlying asset and does so because they anticipate a rise in the value of the underlying; they are "bullish" on the underlying.

Short call: The seller of a call option has the obligation to sell the underlying asset and does so because they anticipate a fall in the value of the underlying; they are "bearish" on the underlying.

Long put: The buyer of a put option has the right to sell an underlying asset and does so because they are bearish on the underlying asset.

Short put: The seller of a put option has the obligation to buy the underlying asset and does so because they are bullish on the underlying asset.

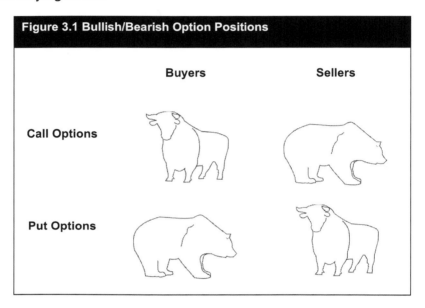

Figure 3.1 Bullish/Bearish Option Positions

Options Premium

To acquire these rights, buyers of options must pay a price called the *option premium* to the seller of the option. Do not confuse this with the exercise price of the option, which is the price at which the underlying asset will be exchanged.

American vs. European Options

- American options may be exercised at any time up to and including the contract's expiration date.

- European options can be exercised only on the contract's expiration date.

The name of the option does not have geographical implications at all. American options are the most commonly traded, while European options are easiest to price.

There are other option types, such as Asian options and Bermudan options, and we will discuss those later in the section on exotic options.

Exchange-Traded vs. Over-The-Counter

Options can be either exchange-traded or over-the-counter (OTC). Exchange-traded options (also called "listed options") have standardized contracts, and are settled through a clearing house with fulfillment guaranteed by the credit of the exchange. Over-the-counter options (also called "dealer options") are traded between two private parties, and are not listed on an exchange. The terms of OTC options are unrestricted and may be individually tailored to meet any requirement. OTC options have more credit risk than exchange-traded options and usually at least one of the counterparties to an OTC option is a well-capitalized institution.

Drawing Options Payoff Diagrams

The payoff diagrams of the four different simple options positions are shown in Figures 3.2–3.6.

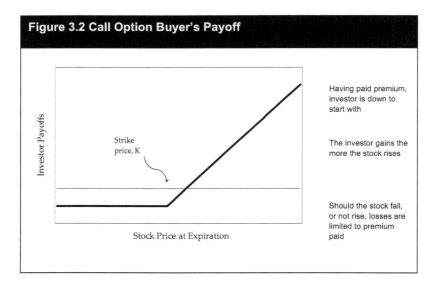

Figure 3.2 Call Option Buyer's Payoff

Investor Payoffs

Strike price, K

Stock Price at Expiration

Having paid premium, investor is down to start with

The investor gains the more the stock rises

Should the stock fall, or not rise, losses are limited to premium paid

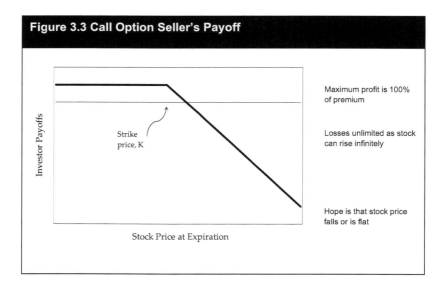

Figure 3.3 Call Option Seller's Payoff

Investor Payoffs

Strike price, K

Stock Price at Expiration

Maximum profit is 100% of premium

Losses unlimited as stock can rise infinitely

Hope is that stock price falls or is flat

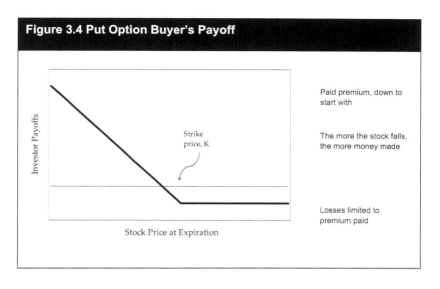

Figure 3.4 Put Option Buyer's Payoff

Investor Payoffs

Strike price, K

Stock Price at Expiration

Paid premium, down to start with

The more the stock falls, the more money made

Losses limited to premium paid

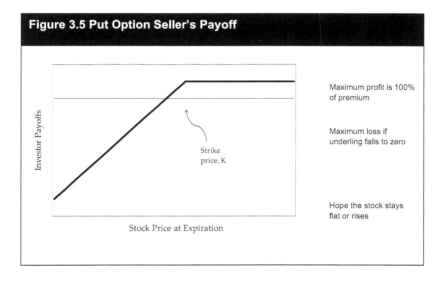

Figure 3.5 Put Option Seller's Payoff

Investor Payoffs

Strike price, K

Stock Price at Expiration

Maximum profit is 100% of premium

Maximum loss if underling falls to zero

Hope the stock stays flat or rises

Combining all of the above diagrams gives us the following diamond-shaped image shown in Figure 3.6, which can be helpful for remembering the four different payoffs. If the option holder benefits more from an up move, there is a bull icon, and if they would benefit more from a down move, there is a bear icon.

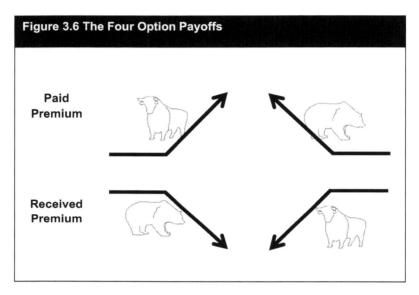

Figure 3.6 The Four Option Payoffs

Paid Premium

Received Premium

Expiration Dates

The Expiration date, is the date on which the options contract concludes, or expires. The option holder must exercise the option on or before the expiry date or allow it to expire worthless. Typically, traded option contracts expire according to a pre-determined calendar. For instance, for US exchange-listed equity option contracts, the expiration date is always the Saturday that follows the third Friday of the month, unless that Friday is a market holiday, in which case the expiration is on the Friday.

The clearing firm may automatically exercise any option that is *in the money* (definition later in this chapter) at expiration to preserve its value for the holder of the option. However the holder may request that the options are not exercised automatically.

Strike Prices

The *strike price* or exercise price of an option is the price at which an option may be exercised. Strike prices are fixed in the option contract. For call options, the strike price is where the security can be bought up to the expiration date, while for put options the strike price is the price at which shares can be sold.

For in the money options, the difference between the underlying security's current market price and the option's strike price represents the amount of profit per share gained upon the exercise of the option.

For exchange-listed options, strike prices are typically spaced at some logical "round number" distance apart, such as $2.50, $5, or $10 price differences between the strikes. Stock splits and stock dividends can result in temporarily irregular strikes.

Intrinsic Value and Time Value of Options

The *intrinsic value* of an option is its value if it was exercised immediately. Thus, if the current price of the underlying security is above the strike price, a call has positive intrinsic value, while a put has zero intrinsic value. Intrinsic value is a straight-forward calculation of the difference between the underlying price now and the option's strike price.

The *time value* of an option is the premium a rational investor would pay in excess of its current intrinsic value, based on its potential to increase in value before expiring. Time value partly arises from the uncertainty of future price movements of the underlying and is also due to the discount rate before the expiration date. European options cannot be exercised before the expiration date, so it is possible for their time value to be negative.

In the money (ITM): Options are considered "in the money" if the option has positive intrinsic value as well as time value. A call option is in the money when the strike price is below the spot price. A put option is in the money when the strike price is above the spot price.

At the money (ATM): Options are considered "at the money" if the strike price is the same as the current spot price of the underlying security. An at the money option has no intrinsic value, only time value.

Out of the money (OTM): Options are considered "out of the money" when they have no intrinsic value. A call option is out of the money when the strike price is above the spot price of the underlying security. A put option is out of the money when the strike price is below the spot price.

Options Underlyings

There are numerous different underlyings that options can be based upon. The Financial Accounting Standards Board (FASB) defines an underlying as "a specified interest rate, security price, commodity price, foreign exchange rate, index of prices or rates, or other variable, including the occurrence or nonoccurrence of a specified event such as a scheduled payment under a contract."

The Treatment of Dividends

The payment of dividends to stockholders impacts options prices. Whenever a stock dividend is paid, the stock price falls by the amount of the dividend. If you owned a stock worth $40 today, and it paid a $1 dividend the next day, assuming all other things equal, the next day you should still have $40 of value, so you would expect to have the $1 dividend and a stock worth $39. The stock has to fall to $39 as the company has paid out $1 in cash per share.

Most companies that pay dividends pay do soon a regular basis, often quarterly. These regular dividends do not cause option strikes to be adjusted. The reason is that the market knows about these dividends well in advance and they automatically get factored into the option's price.

Special Dividends and Options Contracts

Sometimes corporations pay a special one-time dividend—often a large cash amount relative to the stock's price, as a means of returning excess cash to shareholders. These are much less common than ordinary dividends, and in the case of special dividends, an adjustment is made to option strikes. Whenever a special dividend is announced, all call and put strikes are immediately reduced by the amount of the dividend. A good example of this is, on July 20, 2004, Microsoft announced a special $3 cash dividend per share. At the time, the stock was trading at around $30, so this was a rather large one-off dividend as a proportion of the share price. This was classified as a special one-time dividend so the option strikes—calls and puts—were adjusted downward by the amount of the dividend. If you were holding the $30 strike call, it became a $27 strike call. If you were holding the $30 strike put, it also became a $27 strike put. The reason for this is that any adjustment in option strikes is done to assure that option investors are not financially hurt, or unfairly rewarded, because of a one-off but significant corporate action such as a split or a special dividend. This helps maintain the integrity of the options market so that investors can take positions without fearing that they will experience large losses due to unexpected, large unusual corporate actions—instead, they will make gains or losses primarily on the basis of their investment thesis of the stock rising or falling due to fundamentals, or technicals, or economic variables the investor is anticipating.

The Treatment of Stock Splits in Options Contracts

Option strikes are adjusted for stock splits. An n for m stock split causes the stock price to fall to m/n of its prior value. The option strike is adjusted to m/n of the previous value. The number of shares covered by the contract changes to n/m of the previous number of shares covered. This adjustment leaves options neutral pre- and post-split. There is the same treatment for special stock dividends and rights offerings.

For example, in the case of a US stock trading at $90 per share, the company may feel it is optimal to trade in the $30 range, and so announces a 3-for-1 stock split. The holder of a 90 strike call option with the right to buy 100 shares on expiration date now holds a $30 strike call option with the right to buy 300 shares.

What are Options Position Limits?

Position limits are imposed by exchanges for the purpose of maintaining stable and fair markets. These are the highest number of options or futures contracts an investor is allowed to hold on one underlying security. Exchanges and/or regulatory bodies establish different position limits for each contract based on trading volume and underlying share quantity. Exchanges such as the Chicago Board Options Exchange (CBOE) calculate position limits for options transactions. Contracts held by one individual investor with different brokers may be combined in order to accurately gauge the level of control held by one party.

In the aftermath of the financial crisis of 2007-2008, Wall Street reform regulations required the Commodity Futures Trading Commission to establish position limits for commodity futures and swaps. These limits help prevent the market from being unduly influenced by one investor or group of investors.

What is Options Margin?

Margin is collateral that the holder of a financial instrument has to deposit to cover some or all of the credit risk to their counterparty. The collateral can be in the form of cash or securities, and it is deposited in a margin account. Historically, "margin" was originally called *performance bond*. Most of the exchanges today use SPAN (Standard Portfolio Analysis of Risk) methodology for calculation of margin in 'Options' and 'Futures.' SPAN was developed by the Chicago Mercantile Exchange in 1988.

SPAN is based on a sophisticated set of algorithms that determine margin according to a global (total portfolio) assessment of the one-day risk for a trader's account. The SPAN system, through its algorithms, sets the margin of each position to its calculated worst possible one-day move. The system, after calculating the margin of each position, can shift any excess margin on existing positions to new positions or existing positions that are short of margin.

Margin in options trading is the amount of cash deposit needed in an options trading broker account when selling (writing) options. Options margin is required as collateral to ensure the options writer's ability to fulfill the obligations under the options contracts sold.

When you sell call options, you are obliged to sell the underlying to the holder of those call options if the options are exercised. If you don't already own that underlying in your account, you will have to buy it on the open market in order to sell to the holder of those call options if the contract is settled in stock. In order to ensure that you have the money to buy those stocks on the open market when the assignment happens, the options broker will require you to have a certain amount of money in your account on deposit.

Similarly, when you write put options, you are obliged under the contract to buy the underlying from the holder of those put options if the options are exercised. That is why the options broker needs to make sure that you have sufficient funds to buy those stocks from the holder of the put options if the contract amount is assigned.

Long options investors typically just have to pay the entire premium. Because they have paid the full premium and the premium is all they can lose, no additional margin is needed from options buyers as there is no counterparty risk on their side of the transaction.

How Does Options Exercise Work?

The owner of an option contract has the right to exercise it and, thus, require that the transaction specified by the contract is to be carried out immediately between the two parties. Once this has occurred, the option contract is terminated. When exercising a call option, the owner of the option purchases the underlying at the strike price from the option seller, while for a put option, the owner of the option sells the underlying to the option seller, again at the strike price.

The option style, as specified in the contract, determines when, how, and under what circumstances the option holder may exercise it. It is at the discretion of the owner whether and sometimes when to exercise it.

- European style option contracts can only be exercised at the option's expiration date
- American style option contracts can be exercised at any time up to the option's expiration.
- Bermudan style options contracts cay only be exercised on specified dates.

The option contract specifies the manner in which the contract is to be settled.

- Physically settled options require the actual delivery of the underlying. This could be as simple as delivering 100 shares of stock, or involve delivery of a commodity such as oil.

- Cash-settled options do not require the actual delivery of the underlying. Instead, the market value, at the exercise date, of the underlying is compared to the strike price, and the difference is paid by the option seller to the owner of the option. Most listed exchange-traded index options are cash settled.

In the United States, the Options Clearing Corporation (OCC) will automatically exercise any option that is set to expire in the money by 1 cent or more. This is done for the convenience of brokers, who would otherwise have to request exercise of all in the money options. This is known as "exercise by exception." A holder of such options may request that they not be exercised by exception. The price of the underlying security used to determine the need for exercise by exception is the price of the regular-hours trade reported last to the OCC at or before 4:01:30 p.m. ET on the day before expiration. This trade will have occurred during normal trading hours. It can be of any size and come from any participating exchange. The OCC reports this price tentatively at 4:15 pm, but, to allow time for exchanges to correct errors the OCC does not make the price official until 5:30 p.m.

Transaction Costs When Trading Options

Transaction costs are made up of a combination of commissions and the bid/ask spread. Commissions vary from broker to broker, and are usually cheaper for larger accounts than for small accounts. The bid/ask spread is the difference in price at which a market maker is willing to buy an asset from you or sell it to you. For example, if the bid price of a share is $20.07 and the ask price is $20.09 then the "bid/ask spread" is $0.02. When you buy an option, you will pay a commission, and when you close out your position by entering an offsetting trade, you will pay a commission again. If an option is exercised, the commission is the same as if the customer had entered a trade to buy the underlying stock. Thus trading options can be very expensive from a transaction costs perspective, and transaction costs can wipe out any gains a trader may have hoped to make. Because of these high transaction costs, options tend not to be traded very actively by many investors, and they are usually considerably less actively traded than futures.

What are Naked Options Positions?

A *naked position* refers to a situation in which a trader sells an option contract without holding an offsetting position in the underlying security as protection from an adverse shift in price. Naked positions are considered very risky as some positions can, in theory, lead to an unlimited amount of loss. If, for example, the writer of a call option does not own the underlying security, they will be exposed to extreme risk as the price of the underlying could move dramatically higher. In this scenario, the obligation is to sell the underlying to the purchaser at the predetermined strike price. Margin calculations are typically much more favorable to investors who are not "naked" since losses are potentially much higher on naked sales of options.

Certain options traders like to "sell the teenies." This term comes from when stocks used to trade in fractions of a dollar, and a "teenie" was 1/16th of a dollar, which was usually the lowest price at which an option could trade. These traders look for situations where there is a 1/16, or now just a very small, bid for options that have virtually no statistical value and sell them. This sale might normally take place quite close to expiration—within a week or so, or be on a well out of the money option. In many cases, selling these is similar to selling insurance but it has been compared to picking up pennies in front of a steam roller. While this strategy might provide steady income much of the time, generally the one or two cases that do end up losing money might possibly negate long periods of prior positive returns and maybe even cause bankruptcy of the habitual teeny seller.

The Options Clearing House

A clearing house is a financial institution that provides clearing and settlement services for financial securities transactions. A clearing house stands between two member firms and its purpose is to reduce the risk of one or more counterparty failing to honor its trade settlement obligations. A clearing firm, or clearing broker, is distinct from a clearing house. A clearing firm or clearing broker is another term for a brokerage company that provides traders and asset managers access to exchange traded products, where the traders or assets managers do not have direct access to a clearing house to execute their trades. A clearing house reduces the settlement risks by netting offsetting transactions between multiple counterparties, by requiring margin deposits, by providing independent valuation of trades and collateral, by monitoring the credit worthiness of the member firms, and often, by providing a guarantee fund that can be used to cover losses that exceed a defaulting clearing firm's collateral on deposit.

The Options Clearing Corporation (OCC) in the United States was founded in 1973. It is presently the world's largest equity derivatives clearing organization. It provides central counterparty clearing and settlement services to various exchanges and platforms for options, futures, and securities lending transactions. By acting as guarantor, the OCC ensures that the obligations of the contracts they clear are fulfilled.

The OCC operates under the jurisdiction of the Securities and Exchange Commission (SEC) and the Commodity Futures Trading Commission (CFTC). Under its SEC jurisdiction, the OCC clears transactions for put and call options on common stock, stock indexes, foreign currencies, interest rate composites, and single-stock futures. As a registered Derivatives Clearing Organization under CFTC jurisdiction, the OCC offers clearing and settlement services for transactions in futures and options on commodity futures contracts.

The OCC is overseen by a clearing member dominated board of

directors. The OCC operates as an industry utility and receives most of its revenue from clearing fees—a small charge is imposed on every single trade undertaken.

The OCC gets notified of long options holders' intentions to "exercise" their options. Assignment occurs when an option holder notifies their broker, who then notifies the OCC. The OCC then selects, randomly, a member firm who was short the same option contract and notifies the firm. The firm then selects a customer, (either randomly, first-in-first-out, or using some other equitable method) who was short the option, for assignment. That customer is "assigned," requiring them to fulfill the obligation that they agreed to when they wrote the option.

Warrants, Convertible Bonds, and Employee Stock Options

Warrants, convertible bonds, and *employee stock options* have similarities to the listed stock options we have discussed up until now, but differ in that:

1. There are a fixed number issued, whereas with stock options, open interest is unlimited
2. These create dilution, whereas regular listed stock options never create dilution

Warrants are very similar to call options. Warrants confer the same rights as equity options and often can be traded in secondary markets like options. However, there are several key differences between warrants and equity options:

1. Warrants are issued by private parties, typically the corporation on which a warrant is based, rather than a public options exchange.
2. Warrants issued by the company itself are dilutive. When the warrant issued by a company is exercised, the company issues new shares of stock, so the number of outstanding shares

increases. When a call option is exercised, the owner of the call option receives an existing share from an assigned call writer. This is unlike call options traded on public options exchanges, these have no dilutive impacts on the corporation's shares outstanding—they are literally side-bets on the price movements of the shares and cannot increase the firm's total shares outstanding when exercised.

3. A warrant's lifetime is usually measured in years, as long as 15 years, while options are typically measured in months. This is a function of the differing goals of the two issuers. The warrant issuer, the company itself, is trying to raise long-term financing. The options exchanges are providing a forum for investors to place side-bets or hedges based on share price movements.

Convertible bonds are a type of bond that the holder can convert into shares of common stock in the issuing company or cash of equal value, at an agreed-upon price. They are a hybrid security with debt- and equity-like features. They typically have a low coupon, lower than otherwise similar debt the company might issue at that point in time, but they carry additional value through the option to convert the bond to stock, and thereby participate in further growth in the company's equity value. Convertibles are economically equivalent to a bond plus a warrant.

Employee stock options (ESOs) are warrants that are issued as a private contract between an employer and employee. Over the course of employment, a company might generally issue ESOs to an employee which can be exercised at a particular price set on the grant day. Depending on the vesting schedule and the maturity of the options, the employee may elect to exercise the options at some point, obliging the company to sell the employee its stock at whatever stock price was used as the exercise price.

What Affects the Price of an Option?

The main factors impacting the premium price of stock options are:

- The current stock price S_0
- Strike price agreed on   K
- Time to maturity/expiration   T
- Volatility of the stock price σ
- Risk-free interest rate   r
- Dividends expected during option life

The Price of the Underlying

The price of the underlying is the key factor that determines the premium price of an option. The options payoff is the difference between the spot price and the strike price. The price of an option premium for a given strike price will change based on the price of the underlying stock.

Long call options are more valuable when the underlying spot price increases.

Long put options become more valuable when the underlying spot price decreases.

The Strike Price of the Option

The strike price is the contracted price that will be exchanged in the event of the exercise of the option by the option buyer. Hence strike price plays a vital role in determining the premium price of an option. The exercise price will remain the same throughout the life of an option contract and will not undergo any change, with the earlier-noted exceptions of relatively rare corporate actions such as special dividend announcements and stock splits.

Time to Options Expiration

With more time, there is more uncertainty. The more time to expiration, the greater the chance that there will be fluctuation in the price of the underlying to the advantage of one of the parties to the contract. Thus, the greater the time, the higher the time value of the option. An option's premium price is directly related to the time remaining till expiration. The buyer of an option stands to gain if the option contract finishes in the money. If there is more time to expiration, the chance of the option ending in the money is higher. As the time to expiration of an options contract passes, the value of the option erodes.

If an investor buys an option that is one year away from expiration, it will obviously be more expensive than a similar option that is only five minutes away from expiration. All options exhibit time decay and are wasting assets.

The Volatility of the Underlying

The volatility of an options underlying can be seen as a measure of uncertainty about the valuation of the underlying. The standard deviation of the historical price movements of the underlying asset over a defined period of time is typically used to measure the volatility of that asset. The higher the volatility is, the more likely it is that an asset's price will move up or down a lot. Thus, an option on a volatile asset is worth more than an option on an asset with little volatility. If a market becomes more volatile, the premium for option contracts, both puts and calls, would go up. Someone who bought options earlier would benefit if market volatility increases to the detriment of the person who sold the options to them.

The Risk Free Rate

The cost of carry depends on the risk-free rate of interest in the market concerned. The higher the interest rate, the higher the call option price and lower the put option price. The lower the interest rate, the lower the call option price and higher the put option price.

Higher interest rates have two impacts on stock options valuations:

1. Higher expected return on stock
2. The present value of future cash flows of an option decrease

If all else is kept equal, an increase in interest rates increases call prices and decreases put prices.

Expected Cashflows on the Underlying

Stock dividends are paid only to the holder of the underlying security on the record date. Owners of call options on the same underlying stock are not eligible to receive dividends. Dividends paid during the life of an options contract reduce the price of the underlying. This has to be reflected in the price of options.

An announcement of a new dividend or an increase in the dividend of an underlying stock reduces pre-existing market call prices and increases pre-existing market put prices. A surprise announcement of a reduction in a stock's dividends has the effect of increasing pre-existing market call prices and decreasing pre-existing market put prices.

Chapter 3 Questions

1. What is the difference between a call option and a put option?

2. Is there a difference between a long put option and a short put option, or are they the same thing just viewed from a different perspective?

3. Why must options buyers pay a premium? Why do the sellers not have to pay?

4. What is the difference between American and European options?

5. All else being equal, should an American option or a European option be more expensive to buy? Explain.

6. Are European investors able to trade American options?

7. What is an OTC option?

8. Draw the payoff profile of a long call option.

9. Why do options contracts have different strikes and expirations?

10. Explain Intrinsic Value and Time Value.

11. Explain what an at-the-money option is.

12. A trader buys a stock option for $2 with the right to purchase a share of stock for $50. Identify whether this is a put or a call option, what the strike price is, and what the premium is.

13. How do dividends impact options prices and why?

14. What is a special dividend? Are special dividends treated differently to regular dividends?

15. If there is a 3-for-2 stock split, will this affect option strikes? How would it affect an option with a strike price of 40?

16. Why do exchanges impose position limits?

17. Does the options margin requirement take your overall portfolio into account, or just apply to each options position?

18. Do options sellers or buyers typically put up more margin? If so, explain why.

19. What is meant by a naked options position?

20. Explain the role of the clearing house. How does it benefit investors? How is the clearing house financed?

21. What is the difference between a warrant and a call option?

22. What type of option is built into a convertible bond?

23. List the six main factors that impact options prices?

24. Which of the following options positions are bullish, and which are bearish? Long call, short call, long put, short put.

25. Suppose you have purchased a European put on a share for $4. The share price is $51 and the strike on the put is $48. Under which circumstances will you earn a profit? Under what circumstances will the put be exercised? Draw a diagram of the variation in your profit as it changes with the underlying stock price at maturity.

26. A company that has listed stock options trading in the market declares a 2-for-1 stock split. Explain how an investor's position changes if they were, prior to the ex-dividend date, long 1 contract on 100 shares of calls on this company with a strike of $50.

27. Employee stock options are different from publicly traded, exchange-listed options because they alter a company's capital structure. Explain this mechanism.

Chapter 4

OPTIONS TRADING STRATEGIES

In the last chapter we looked at the payoffs of individual options. Now we will look at the effect of combining various options with each other and with the underlying asset.

Assumptions and notation: For the purposes of this chapter we will be assuming that there are no transaction costs involved in trading, a consistent tax environment, and that all borrowing and lending occurs at the same interest rate (r). These assumptions significantly simplify options valuation modeling, although they are somewhat unrealistic vis-à-vis the actual trading environment.

We will be using the same notation as before for S_0, K, T, S_T, and r

In addition:

- C will stand for the value of an American call option on 1 share
- P will stand for the value of an American put option on 1 share
- c will stand for the value of a European call option on 1 share
- p will stand for the value of an European put option on 1 share

There are a number of option strategies that involve trading a single option and its underlying asset as a combination.

What is a Covered Call?

Many investors who are long a stock are willing to sell away some of its upside, by selling a call option on that stock. This is known as a *covered call*, or sometimes called a buy-write. The long position in the underlying instrument is said to provide the "cover" since the shares can be delivered to the buyer of the call if the option buyer decides to exercise.

Suppose an investor is long a stock, and they feel it will rise, but not more than, for example, 5% in a given month. In such a scenario, they will be happy to sell a one-month expiry call with a strike 5% above the current share price and thus earn the option premium. If the stock rises more than 5% in that month, the investor will have only captured a gain of 5% because option will have been exercised, plus the option premium. However, if the stock rises a little, stays flat, or even falls, they will have the same share position they originally had, plus they will have earned the option premium. This is a very popular strategy for long-only investors, which comprise a huge proportion of the investment space, and there are many investment funds devoted to investing in just this strategy.

The payoff of the individual components of a covered call strategy looks like Figure 4.1.

Like every investment strategy, this is not without risk. One of the difficulties of this strategy is that, suppose, like our investor above, you were bullish on a stock, and owned the stock as a long-term holding, and you decide to sell the 5% upside strike 1-month expiry call, estimating that the stock is unlikely to gain as much as 5% in the coming one-month timeframe, and accept a small premium, for example less than 1% of the stock value, from the option sale. If the company is announced to be the target of a takeover offer within that next month, the shares are likely to rise 30% or more instantly, and you will be exercised against at the option's expiry, gaining only 6% when your underlying thesis—being bullish on the company— was accurate and could have earned you a very quick 30% gain.

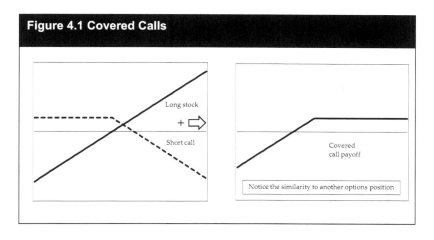

Figure 4.1 Covered Calls

Long stock

+

Short call

Covered call payoff

Notice the similarity to another options position

Another problem with the buy-write strategy is if you continue holding a long position in the underlying stock and sell calls alongside it, but then you lose conviction in your long position after you have sold the call. In this scenario, you may be reluctant to incur all of the transaction costs to unwind both the long stock position and the short call positions. In many cases, buy-write portfolio managers will prefer to simply hold the position to expiry instead of "crossing the spread" to exit the option position. If the stock falls considerably by the time of the options expiry, the gain from the option premium of ~1% may be dwarfed by the losses in a stock you have lost conviction in.

What is a Protective Put?

A *protective put* is a portfolio strategy where an investor is long an underlying and buys enough put options to cover that position. The resulting portfolio has a potentially unlimited upside due to the theoretically unlimited upside of the stock, with limited downside. Of course, one must pay for this through the premium for the put. This strategy can hedge, or insure, a position in a stock. The buyer of a put protects themselves from a drop in the stock price below the strike price of the put. In the event that the put expires worthless, the buyer has lost only the option premium paid for the put. If the stock moves up a lot, the investor will have made less money than had they been long the stock alone. The difference will be the amount of the put premium.

The payoff of the individual components of a protective put strategy looks like this: This options strategy is economically identical to being long a call on the underlying asset. However, for various reasons, it may be preferable for the investor to hold the position in this manner. It could be that they prefer to be long the stock over a very long timeframe, this will in many jurisdictions also be tax-advantageous to the investor, without having traded in and out of the stock via various options exercises that may occur over time. Also, the investor may choose to only purchase the puts on occasional, or periodic, bases at points when they feel the market or the individual stock risk is temporarily heightened, or at points where they feel that puts are more affordable, and this will protect their portfolio.

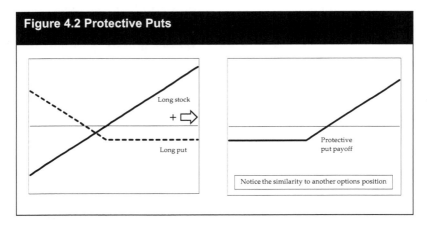

What is a Covered Put?

The *covered put* strategy is just the opposite of the covered call strategy. An investor sells short the underlying to cover a short put option position. The covered put strategy is a neutral to bearish strategy because the investor is expecting the underlying to go down or stay neutral. If the stock drops, the investor will have the underlying put to them at the strike price, which covers the short position they had in the underlying. The investor keeps the initial premium received from selling the put. If the underlying price rises, the investor keeps the premium, but they are still holding the short position and could sustain a loss if the underlying rallies a lot. They will lose less money than had they been short the underlying alone, the difference being the premium received. Note that the net position you are left with is identical to a short call option. This is considered a highly risky position given that you have unlimited downside exposure should the underlying asset rise significantly. Having collected a small amount of premium from selling a put option would offer a very small mitigation in the event of a significant rise in the underlying, in most cases.

The payoff of the individual components of a covered put strategy looks like Figure 4.3.

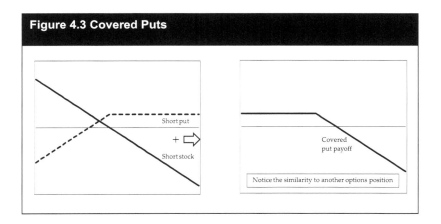

Figure 4.3 Covered Puts

Short put

Short stock

Covered put payoff

Notice the similarity to another options position

What is a Protective Call?

A *protective call* is a trading strategy in which you sell short the underlying, and buy a call option in order to protect that position. It is the exact opposite of a protective put. The resulting portfolio has a large upside as the stock could fall all the way to zero, while limiting the downside. Of course, one must pay for this through the premium for the call. An investor may use this strategy to hedge, or insure, a short position in an underlying. The call protects the trader from the potentially unlimited rise in the price of the underlying. In the event that the call expires worthless, the buyer has lost only the option premium paid for the call. If the underlying falls a lot, the investor will have made less money than had they been short the stock alone. The difference will be the amount of the call premium.

The payoff of the individual components of a protective call strategy looks like Figure 4.4.

In each of the above strategy diagrams, we have asked if the combination payoffs look like other option payoffs. In figure 4.4, note the payoff of a protective call looks just like the payoff of a long put option. Each of the combinations that we have looked at here for options and their underlying gives us a synthetic version of another option. Figure 4.1 demonstrates a covered call gives rise to an exposure equivalent to a short put option. Figure 4.2 demonstrates a protective put gives rise to an equivalent exposure to a long call option. Figure 4.3 demonstrates a covered put gives rise to an exposure equivalent to a short call option.

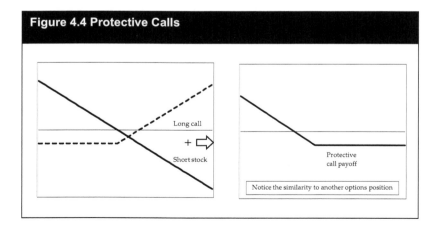

Figure 4.4 Protective Calls

Long call
+
Short stock

Protective call payoff

Notice the similarity to another options position

What is Put Call Parity?

There is a formula that explains all of the relationships we have looked at above, and it is the *put call parity* formula. In financial mathematics, put call parity defines a relationship between the price of a European call option and European put option with the identical strike price and expiration. Put call parity requires a liquid, tradable underlying in order to hold. Put call parity requires minimal assumptions compared to other commonly used financial models.

Two portfolios that always have the same payoff at time T must have the same value at any prior time. Suppose for arguments sake that one portfolio is cheaper than another at a given time. A trader could purchase the cheaper portfolio and go short the more expensive one. At maturity time T, our overall portfolio would, for any value of the share price, have zero value as all of the assets and liabilities would cancel out. Thus, the profit we made at initiation of a trade, time t, would be a riskless profit.

The formula for put call parity is:

$$p + S_0 = c + Ke^{(-rT)}$$

This relationship holds for European options only. If ever the relationship did not exist, there would be arbitrage opportunities for investors to profitably exploit.

Put call parity implies the equivalence of calls and puts. Parity implies that a call option and a put option can be used interchangeably in any delta-neutral portfolio (see discussion on "delta" in Chapter 8). Selling a call while long shares of stock is the same as selling a put. Equivalence of calls and puts is very important when trading options.

Put call parity also implies that in the absence of dividends or other costs of carry, such as when a stock is difficult to borrow or sell short, the implied volatility of calls and puts must be identical. Implied volatility refers to a figure which is backed out of market pricing of options, more specifically, it is the market-implied expectation of the risk, or standard deviation, of the underlying asset's returns over the timeframe of a given market-traded option.

If the underlying pays dividends, the put call parity formula is as follows:

$$p + S_0 = c + Ke^{(-rT)} + Divs \times e^{(-rT)}$$

What are Synthetic Options?

When listed options were first introduced, only call options were made available. Option traders who wished to speculate on the downside while limiting upside risk needed to create the payoff characteristics of put options. They did this by buying call options and simultaneously shorting the underlying. The combination of call options and short stocks creates a synthetic put option, or a position with the exact characteristics of a put option.

This relationship is governed by the principle of Put Call Parity.

There are six basic synthetic positions using put options, call options, and the underlying.

1. Synthetic Long Stock = Long Call + Short Put
2. Synthetic Short Stock = Short Call + Long Put
3. Synthetic Long Call = Long Stock + Long Put
4. Synthetic Short Call = Short Stock + Short Put
5. Synthetic Short Put = Short Call + Long Stock
6. Synthetic Long Put = Long Call + Short Stock

In order for the relationship to work, all options used must be of the same expiration and strike price.

Options Combination Trading Strategies

For the rest of this chapter we will look at a variety of strategies that an options trader can follow using combinations of different options, the underlying, and the risk-free interest rate. The first group of strategies we will look at are spreads.

Options spreads are the basic building blocks of many options trading strategies. A spread position is entered by buying and selling options of the same class on the same underlying security but with different strike prices or expiration dates.

If a spread profits from a rise in the price of the underlying security, it is called a *bull spread*. If a favorable outcome is obtained when the price of the underlying security falls, it is called a *bear spread*.

Bull Spreads

A *bull spread* is a vertical spread options strategy that is designed to profit from a moderate rise in the price of the underlying security. A vertical spread refers to an options strategy of purchasing more than one put option or call option on an underlying asset with the same expiration date, but with different strike prices. Because of put-call parity, a bull spread can be constructed using either put options or call options. If constructed using calls, it is a *bull call spread*; if constructed using puts, it is a *bull put spread*.

A bull call spread is assembled by buying a call option with a low exercise price, and selling another call option with a higher exercise price. Often the call with the lower exercise price will be at the money (ATM), while the call with the higher exercise price will be out of the money (OTM). Both calls must have the same underlying security and expiration date.

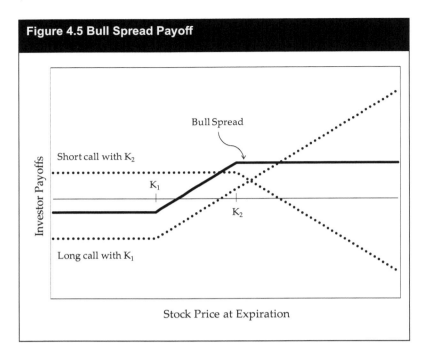

In Figure 4.5, the dotted lines show the payoff profiles of the two individual options. The heavy line shows the combination's payoff.

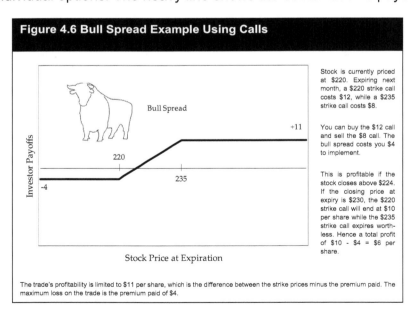

The buyer of the bull spread illustrated in Figure 4.6 pays $4, the seller receives $4. The buyer is bullish and needs the stock to move up $4 or more. The seller is bearish or neutral and wishes the stock to be unchanged or to fall.

A bull spread can also be constructed using puts. This is done by purchasing one put option and simultaneously selling another with a higher strike price on the same underlying security with the same expiration date. The options trader employing this strategy hopes that the price of the underlying security goes up far enough so that the written put options expire worthless.

Bear Spreads

A *bear spread* is a vertical spread options strategy that can be used when the options trader is moderately bearish on the underlying security. Because of put-call parity, a bear spread can be assembled using either puts or calls. If you use calls, it is known as a *bear call spread*; if you use puts, it is known as a *bear put spread*.

A bear call spread is a limited profit, limited risk options trading strategy that can be used when the options trader is moderately bearish on the underlying security. It is entered by buying call options of a certain strike price and selling the same number of call options of lower strike price on the same underlying security with the same expiration date.

A bear put spread is similar, it is entered by buying one put option and selling the same number of lower strike price put options on the same underlying security with the same expiration date. The trader hopes that the price of the underlying drops, maximizing profit when the underlying drops below the strike price of the written option, netting the difference between the strike prices less the premium paid.

In Figure 4.7, the dotted lines show the payoff profiles of the two individual options. The heavy line shows the combination's payoff.

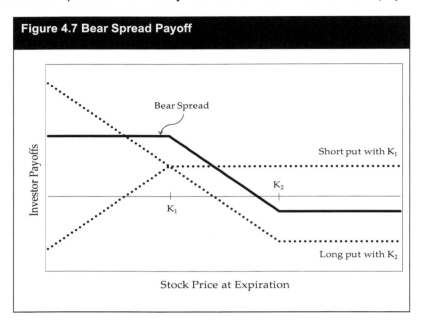

Figure 4.7 Bear Spread Payoff

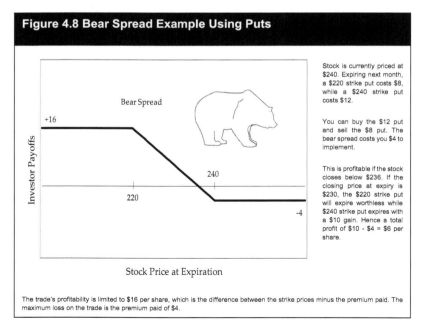

Figure 4.8 Bear Spread Example Using Puts

Stock is currently priced at $240. Expiring next month, a $220 strike put costs $8, while a $240 strike put costs $12.

You can buy the $12 put and sell the $8 put. The bear spread costs you $4 to implement.

This is profitable if the stock closes below $236. If the closing price at expiry is $230, the $220 strike put will expire worthless while $240 strike put expires with a $10 gain. Hence a total profit of $10 - $4 = $6 per share.

The trade's profitability is limited to $16 per share, which is the difference between the strike prices minus the premium paid. The maximum loss on the trade is the premium paid of $4.

The buyer of the bear spread illustrated in Figure 4.8 pays $4, the seller receives $4. The buyer is bearish and wants the stock to fall $4 or more. The seller is bullish or neutral, wanting the stock to rise or be unchanged.

Butterfly Spreads

A *butterfly spread* is a limited risk, non-directional options strategy. The trader sells two option contracts at the middle strike price and buys one option contract at a lower strike price and one option contract at a higher strike price. This is called a long butterfly spread. Either puts or calls can be used for a butterfly spread.

The maximum payoff is when the stock price at expiration equals the strike price of the written options. Therefore, the strategy can be made neutral-bullish or neutral-bearish by slightly increasing or decreasing all of the strike prices by the same amount.

The butterfly requires four options, and the transaction costs can often exceed the profits. Therefore, the spread is commonly used by professional traders who have very low transaction costs and build it with what they consider "mispriced" options to increase the payoff.

Figure 4.9 shows the payoff of a butterfly spread. The dotted lines are the individual options and the black line is the payoff of the overall position.

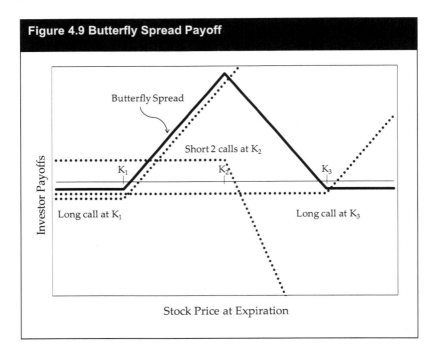

Figure 4.9 Butterfly Spread Payoff

Calendar Spreads

An options spread established by simultaneously entering a long and short position on the same underlying asset but with different expiration months is called a *calendar spread*. The calendar spread can be used to attempt to take advantage of a difference in the implied volatilities between two different months' options. The trader will ordinarily implement this strategy when the options they are buying have a distinctly lower implied volatility than the options they are selling.

An example of a calendar spread would be to buy a call option with a given strike price K and time to expiration and write a second call option with the same strike price but a shorter time to expiration.

If the trader buys a nearby month's options in some underlying market and sells that same underlying market's further-out options of the same strike price, this is known as a *reverse calendar spread*.

Straddles

A *straddle* is an options strategy where the investor holds a position in both a call and put with the same strike price and expiration date. It is called a *long straddle* if you buy both the call and put, and a *short straddle* if you sell both. This is a strategy an investor might pursue if they believe that a stock's price would move significantly, but they are unsure of the direction. Because of the amount of premium they are spending, the stock price must move significantly to make this strategy profitable. Should only a small movement in price occur in either direction, the investor will experience a loss. When stocks are expected to jump, such as when they have a big announcement coming out, the market tends to price options at a higher premium. This reduces the expected payoff of this strategy, and in order for it to be profitable, the move needs to be quite a surprise, and quite significant.

Straddles are typically traded using at the money options. Although buying a call and a put at the same strike is defined as a straddle, buying them far away from the money does not give you a targeted exposure—a payoff based on a large move from the current underlying price either up or down.

Payoff diagrams for straddles are shown in Figures 4.10 and 4.11.

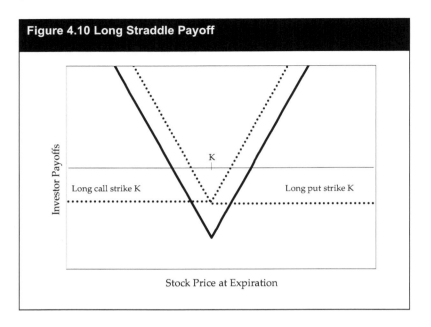

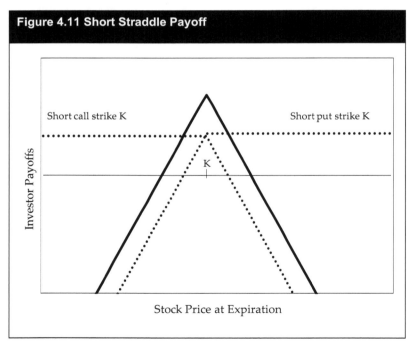

Strangles

A *strangle* is an options strategy where the investor holds a position in both a call and put with different strike prices but with the same maturity and underlying asset. It allows the holder to profit based on how much the price of the underlying security moves, with relatively minimal exposure to the direction of price movement. When you buy the put and call it is known as a *long strangle*, while selling them is known as a *short strangle*. A strangle is similar to a straddle, but involves buying an out-of-the-money call option and an out-of-the-money put option. A strangle is generally less expensive than a straddle for this reason.

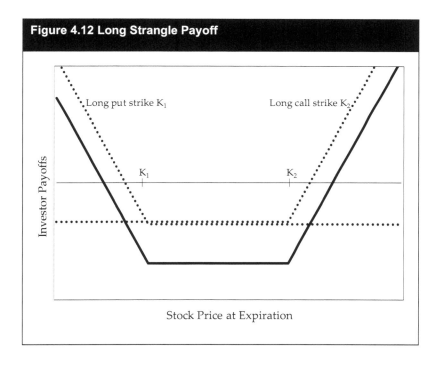

Figure 4.12 Long Strangle Payoff

Risk Reversals

A *risk reversal* is an options strategy that involves selling an out-of-the-money put and simultaneously buying an out-of-the-money call, both with the same maturity. Often traders will look at the "25 risk reversal" which is the volatility of the 25 delta (out of the money) call less the volatility of the 25 delta (out of the money) put for a given maturity (see discussion on "delta" in Chapter 8). The risk reversal is a less-used strategy in equity options, but is quite common in currency and commodities options.

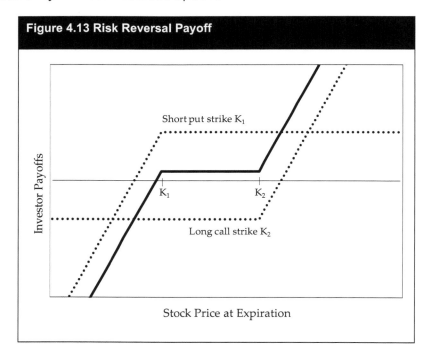

Figure 4.13 Risk Reversal Payoff

Short put strike K_1

K_1 K_2

Long call strike K_2

Investor Payoffs

Stock Price at Expiration

Risk reversal prices are also used as an investor sentiment gauge and as a measure of *volatility skew*. When a risk reversal position is selling for a net debit, it means that out-of-the-money call options are more expensive than out of the money put options. This occurs when the implied volatility of the call options is greater than the implied volatility of the put options. . When a risk reversal position is selling for a net credit (also known as a "Negative Risk Reversal"), it means that out-of-the-money put options are more expensive than similarly out of the money call options, meaning investors are more concerned about a large drop than a large price gain. These prices imply a skewed distribution of expected spot returns. In currency options trading, risk reversals are directly quoted based on implied volatility so that it is even easier to see investor sentiment.

Financial institutions often find themselves as net sellers of puts and calls to their customers. The traders at these banks usually do not have strong views about market direction and will only sell these options if they feel that the premium they are charging is sufficient such that after all hedging expenses, which includes the use of the banks resources and all transaction costs, they will turn a profit. According to the OCC 2015 data, 71% of options positions are closed our prior to expiry, 7% are exercised, and 22% expire worthless. Option sellers are often considered to have better odds than option buyers for positions held until expiration. However, it is worth noting that it is possible to have 90% of your trades win, but to lose a greater amount on the remaining 10% of your trades; the majority of options are closed out prior to expiration; and many investors are delta-hedgers. Delta-hedgers include nearly all investment bank-based market-makers of options (they generally do not have the mandate to take "bets" on the direction of implied volatility for their trading, instead they are mandated to provide liquidity and maintain neutrality of their position via delta-hedging their positions continually. Delta-hedgers would also include most volatility arbitrage traders, these portfolio managers are seeking to profit from perceived "mispricings" in implied volatilies of traded options, but in order to crystallize profits around these mispricings, they must delta-hedge their options positions. Option sellers need not be more profitable than option buyers given uneven win/loss size ratios, variable delta-hedging results, and the proportion of options not live until expiration.

The CBOE maintains a number of indices that you can find on their website showing the returns of a variety of simple options strategies. Figure 4.14 shows a list of some of the more popular options strategies.

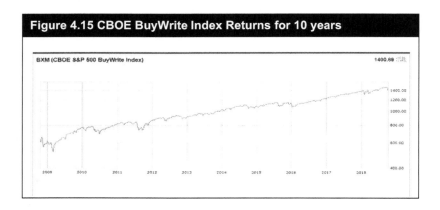

Figure 4.14 CBOE Option Strategy Indices

Index	Ticker	Hold stocks or cash	S&P 500 1 month	S&P 500 3 Month	Start Date
S&P 500 BuyWrite	BXM	S&P 500 stocks	ATM call options	None	Jun-1986
S&P 500 2% OTM BuyWrite	BXY	S&P 500 stocks	2% OTM calls	None	Jun-1988
S&P 500 PutWrite	PUT	US T-bills	ATM put options	None	Jun-1986
S&P 500 95-110 Collar	CLL	S&P 500 stocks	110% OTM calls	95% OTM puts	Jun-1986

Figure 4.15 CBOE BuyWrite Index Returns for 10 years

BXM (CBOE S&P 500 BuyWrite Index)   1400.69

Figure 4.15 shows a ten-year chart of the returns of the CBOE's BXM BuyWrite Index.

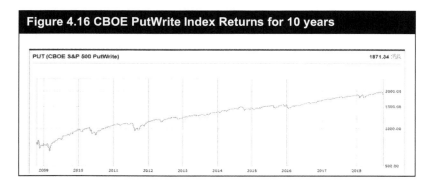

Figure 4.16 CBOE PutWrite Index Returns for 10 years

PUT (CBOE S&P 500 PutWrite)   1871.34

Figure 4.16 shows a chart of the returns of PUT, the CBOE's PutWrite Index.

Updated charts on the returns of these strategies can be found on the CBOE website, and much more academic research online on the returns of various options trading strategies using resources such as ssrn.com and Google scholar.

Chapter 4 Questions

1. Using put call parity, what options strategy is similar to a covered call?

2. Why might an investor wish to buy a protective put?

3. Does put call parity hold for both American and European options?

4. Suppose there are three different call options available on the same underlying stock with the same expiration. You bought a call with an exercise price of $40, bought a call with an exercise price of $30, and sold two calls with an exercise price of $35. What position have you created? Graph its payoff at maturity. What is the payoff of this position at maturity if the underlying stock price is at $90? What is the lowest value this position could have at maturity, and for what range of stock prices?

5. XYZ stock is priced at $100. At-the-money calls and puts are available on XYZ with the same expiration and are priced at $5 and $4 respectively. Graph the payout at expiration for being long the call and short the put. How does this payout compare to being long the stock?

6. A trader buys a call option with a strike of $50, and a put option with a strike of $45, both with the same maturity. The call costs $3 and the put costs $4. Draw a diagram with the trader's profit versus the underlying's price. What is the options combination called?

7. What is the impact of an unexpected announcement of a cash dividend prior to the maturity of (a) a call option price, and (b) a put option price?

8. European put and call options both with a strike of $40 maturing in 3 months are selling for $3. The risk-free rate is 5%, the

stock's current price is $19, and it will be paying a $1 dividend in one month. Identify the arbitrage opportunity open to a trader.

9. What is meant by a protective put? What options combination is equivalent to a protective put?

10. Draw a diagram showing the variation of an investor's profit and loss with the stock price at expiration for a portfolio consisting of (a) one share and a short position in one call option, (b) two shares and a short position in one call option, (c) one share and a short position in two call options, and (d) one share and a short position in four call options? In each case, assume the call option has an exercise price equal to the current stock price?

11. A stock trades at $95, an at-the-money call option on this stock costs $8 and an at-the-money put option on this stock costs $11. A risk-free zero coupon bond will mature at $100 in one year when the options expire. What should the price of this bond be? Explain.

12. You bought a bear spread with puts on a stock that have exercise prices of $45 and $50 and you also bought a bull spread with puts on the same stock that have exercise prices of $40 and $45. What will this total position be worth if the stock price at expiration is $52? Is there a name for the total position?

Chapter 5

PRICING FINANCIAL OPTIONS

Up until now we have looked at how options work and how they can be combined. We have mentioned options premium and how it is made up of time value and intrinsic value. In this chapter we will look at a few of the most common methods for pricing options. The value of options depends on a number of different variables in addition to the value of the underlying asset. They are complex to value and there are many pricing models in use. All models essentially incorporate the concepts of rational pricing, intrinsic value, time value, and put-call parity.

In this chapter we will give you some insight as to how different variables affect option prices, and we hope to show you that while these methods are extremely useful, they are quite fallible, and can only give you an indication of fair value that is extremely dependent on the inputs into the formulas. The old "garbage in, garbage out" adage is particularly applicable to derivatives valuation—and most of financial mathematics. The formulas we will look at are only as good as the numbers that are put into them and often rely on a number of assumptions that do not always hold up in live securities market trading. They all rely on an estimate of volatility, and on an assumed distribution, that cannot be known in advance.

In general, standard option valuation models depend on the following factors:

- The current market price of the underlying security
- The strike price of the option
- The cost of holding a position in the underlying security, including interest and dividends
- The time to expiration together with any restrictions on when exercise may occur
- An estimate of the future volatility of the underlying security's price over the life of the option.

The Economic Utility of Options Contracts

Options, or option-like contracts have been around for hundreds of years. Only in the 1970s was a formal pricing model introduced..

Options contracts are very similar to insurance contracts, and so most of the ideas used to price them came from the insurance business. As early as 1350 in Palermo, insurance contracts were common for casualty and credit risks relating to shipping. The two kinds of insurance were often being written separately. A popular contract was a *conditional sale* (similar to a put option) where the insurer agreed to purchase ship or cargo if it failed to arrive.

An article in the Economist from May 2, 1885, entitled "The Virtues and Vices of Options" on the flourishing options, or "privileges," markets in Paris and New York tells us: "From the standpoint of business morality, two things may be adduced in connection with options, one for and one against. In the first place, they foster a form of speculation which already flourishes too abundantly. … On the other hand, used by experienced speculators, options are generally great safeguards against unexpected and violent movements in prices…"

This alludes to the ongoing debate among regulators, market practitioners, and investment managers about the "correct" and "moral" role that derivatives play in the financial marketplace. They can be great risk-spreaders, enhancing and enabling commerce to flourish in ways that people might never have imagined—if at various points some form of insurance were not available for purchase. But they can also be vehicles for tremendously levered, concentrated risks and losses that spread out to other counterparties and can damage a much wider range of market participants. This remains as true now as it is did when the Economist opined on it in 1885.

A Short History of Financial Option Pricing

In the case of an insurance company insuring a merchant's ship, through the earlier mentioned conditional sale contract, the insurer agreed to purchase the ship or cargo if it failed to arrive. The insurer would try to assign a probability to the ship sinking, and multiply this by the cost of paying out in this eventuality.

As you can imagine, in order to avoid bankruptcy, insurers put a lot of work into tracking shipping outcomes and developed statistical models to make sure that their assessment of risk was accurate. They would take into account the time of year a journey was being made, the length of time a ship spent at sea, the experience of the captain, the perishability of the cargo, and which ports were being visited. They would also take into account the prices other insurers were charging (see Figure 5.1).

Once insurers got skilled at assessing the risk of a contract, they would then aim to diversify as much as possible so that the law of large numbers would make their overall insurance portfolio profitable.

So how does this relate to options markets where mathematical formulas such as the Black-Scholes model (discussed in the next chapter) are used to price options? The answer is that, as mentioned above, options have been around a lot longer than the

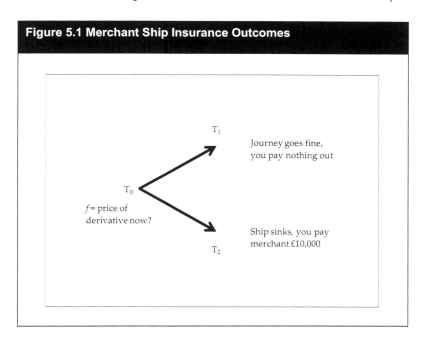

Figure 5.1 Merchant Ship Insurance Outcomes

T_1

Journey goes fine, you pay nothing out

T_0

f = price of derivative now?

Ship sinks, you pay merchant £10,000

T_2

formulas used to price them have been, and options traders still were able to come up with prices to trade at that were mutually acceptable to both buyers and sellers. Like early insurance markets, options sellers did their best to analyze probabilities of various outcomes to determine fair values for options that also included a reasonable profit in order to compensate them for taking the risk.

Louis Bachelier

Louis Bachelier (1870–1946) was a French mathematician credited with being the first person to model the stochastic process now called Brownian motion, which was part of his PhD thesis "The Theory of Speculation," published in 1900. His thesis, which discussed the use of Brownian motion to evaluate stock options, is historically the first paper to use advanced mathematics in the study of finance. Thus, Bachelier is considered a pioneer in the study of financial mathematics and stochastic processes. Bachelier's thesis was not well received because it attempted to apply mathematics to an unfamiliar area for mathematicians.

The Payoff at Expiration: A Starting Point for Pricing Options

We know the fair value of an options contract at expiration based upon the payoff diagrams, see Figure 5.2.

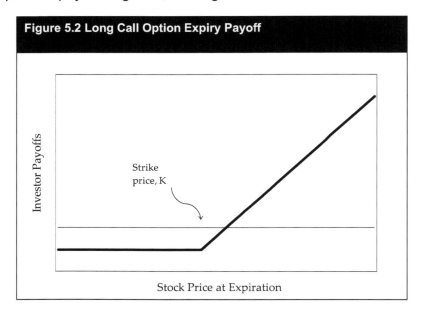

Figure 5.2 Long Call Option Expiry Payoff

We know that options are worth more than their value at expiration before the expiration date due to time value.

Option value = Intrinsic value + Time value

Before mathematical formulas existed for pricing options we knew that the fair value of options was higher than intrinsic value, as there was still time for the underlying to move in your favor, but not how much higher the price should be. Option prices, like all market prices, were just a capital weighted average of every market participant's best guess as to what fair value should be. Should an investor feel that option prices were too high, they could simply sell some options, and this would push the price down to where other investors felt they were too cheap and thus were willing to buy them.

Figure 5.3 highlights the difference in option value pre-expiration and at expiration, the difference being time value.

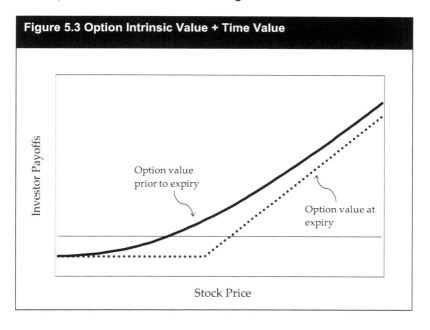

Figure 5.3 Option Intrinsic Value + Time Value

Chapter 5 Questions

1. What pieces of information do you need to know in order to price an American option?

2. How did traders price options before options pricing formulas before formal, mathematically-derived options models existed?

3. Why is Louis Bachelier considered a pioneer in the study of financial mathematics?

4. If a call option with a strike of $100 is trading at a $4 premium and the underlying stock price is $103, what is the time value of this option and what is the intrinsic value of this option? Explain.

5. If a put option with a strike of $100 is trading at a $3 premium and the underlying stock price is $103, what is the time value of this option and what is the intrinsic value of this option? Explain.

6. Why do options have time value?

Chapter 6

LATTICE BASED PRICING MODELS

In finance, lattice models can be applied to the valuation of derivatives, where a discrete time model is required. A simple example would be the pricing of an American option, where the option owner has the right but not the obligation to exercise the option at any time up to and including the maturity date.

The Binomial Tree

The *Binomial Tree* model for valuing options[4] is widely used because it handles a variety of conditions that other models cannot easily do. The Binomial Tree can price an option that incorporates a potentially very flexible evolution of the underlying's behavior over time. As a consequence, it is used to value American options that are exercisable at any time in a given interval as well as Bermudan options that are exercisable at specific instances of time. The model is readily implementable in computer software and spreadsheets. The model uses a "discrete-time" (lattice-based—time described in measurable increments) model of the varying price over time of the underlying.

Although computationally slower than the *Black-Scholes* formula, it

---

[4] First proposed by Cox, Ross and Rubinstein in 1979.

is more accurate, particularly for longer-dated options or securities with dividend payments. For these reasons, versions of the binomial model are widely used by practitioners in the options markets.

The Binomial Tree approach to options pricing involves constructing a diagram of the possible paths of the stock price over the life of the option and then calculating the present value of the final cash flows to determine the current option price.

We will start with a simplified view of the world to explain the approach, then we will slowly adjust the model to make it more and more realistic.

What is the Portfolio Approach to Valuing Options?

The price of a stock today is based on the weighted probabilities of its price in the future. If market participants believe a stock is expected to rise to $70 in the upside scenario in one month with a 60% probability, or to fall to $30 in a downside scenario with a 40% probability, then the stock's expected price in one month is ($70 × 0.6) + ($30 × 0.4) = $54. An investor will pay $54 minus an appropriate discount rate for that stock today. An assessment of the fair value of this stock instrument today therefore includes an assumption of an appropriate risk-factor or discount rate. The assignment of this discount factor will differ across investors—some will perceive this to be a riskier stock investment and others a less-risky stock investment. This gives rise to one element of uncertainty as to the "exact" or "appropriate" stock price at any given moment in time—it relates to the investor's own estimates or measures of an appropriate "return" percentage for taking on the risk of the cash flow uncertainties in the future.

Suppose, however, that an investor holds a portfolio comprised of a stock as well as an option on that same underlying stock. Again, they believe that in an upside scenario the stock will rise to $70, and in a downside scenario it will fall to $30 within one month. Suppose they do not intend to liquidate either leg of this trade earlier than in one month, when the option expires.

Suppose an investor holds some proportion Δ of the stock (see Chapter 8 for definition), and is short one call option on that stock (note that we can configure a similar scenario with puts). Suppose the call option is European, has a strike of $50, and matures in 1 month. At maturity, the investor will have paid out $20 from the short call and hold $\Delta\times70$ of shares in the upside scenario. In the downside scenario, the investor will have $0 cash flow from the call and hold $\Delta\times30$ of shares. Is there a value of Δ, the amount of shares held in the investor's portfolio, where the investor's upside scenario holdings at maturity or downside holdings in one month are equivalent (Figure 6.1)?

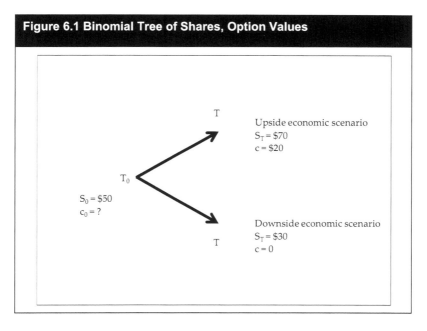

Figure 6.1 illustrates a simple binomial tree. The diagram shows the portfolio at inception next to time T_0. The upward arrow's termination is referred to as the "up node", where the portfolio is reevaluated assuming a time period T has elapsed, with an upward move in the underlying asset's value. The downward arrow's

termination Is referred to as the "down node". The down node illustrates the portfolio assuming a time period T has elapsed, but instead analyses the portfolio's component valuations in the alternate scenario where a downward move in the underlying asset's value occurs.

If we set the upside scenario portfolio holdings equal to the downside scenario holdings, $\Delta70 - \$20 = \$0 + \Delta30$ solving for Δ gives us 0.5. This means that if an investor is short one call option on a share of this company's stock as well as being long half a share of the underlying in their portfolio, they will have a specific outcome in one month, in either an upside or a downside economic scenario. Hence, we can say that this portfolio is a riskless one (the outcomes are known with no uncertainty whatsoever), as shown in Figure 6.2.

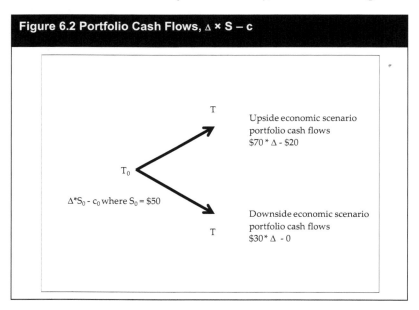

Figure 6.2 Portfolio Cash Flows, $\Delta \times S - c$

In this case, given that we have now constructed a portfolio in which the cash flows are "riskless," we can discount the future cash flows using a risk-free rate and know the value of the portfolio today. If we know the value of one of the instruments, the stock or the call option, we can perfectly value the other instrument. In practice, the price of a publicly traded stock is known at time zero (now) with no uncertainty, so this method enables us to value the call option today, without resorting to any assumptions about the discounting rates of return that different investors would seek if investing in the stock of the company in question, an unknowable figure. An interesting result of this method is that we also do not need to know the probabilities of occurrence of the upside or downside scenarios for the future stock prices in order to calculate the derivative's value. Our former assumptions that the stock has a 60% probability of rising and a 40% probability of falling were not necessary to achieve the valuation result for the option.

We can discount the riskless cash flows at maturity, $30 × 0.5, by the risk-free rate to calculate the value of the portfolio at time zero. If the risk-free rate is 5%, over the one month timeframe, we have that $e^{(-rT)}$ × $30 × 0.5 = 0.5 × 50 − c, solving for c we get that the current value of the call option is 10.06 [0.5 × 50-$e^{(-0.05 \times (1/12))}$ × 30 × 0.5 = 10.06237].

So far, we have found the interesting result that if we know the two next possible steps in an underlying asset's price and we know the risk-free interest rate, we can price a derivative over that timeframe on that underlying.

Our first assumption of only two possible share prices at the end of three months is quite unrealistic, but as you will see, we can keep working with this approach and make more reasonable, real-life assumptions as the chapter progresses.

Notation

This is the notation that we will be using for the rest of this book.

S_0 = spot price of underlying at time zero

f = derivative value at time zero

f_u = derivative value at up node

S_0u =   underlying price at up node

f_d =   derivative value at down node

S_0d =   underlying price at down node

As we move forward with binomial valuations, underpinning the concept is that you can create a portfolio at each node knowing that some value of Δ of the underlying makes the portfolio cash flows equivalent at time T. It is important to note that we are not valuing the option in absolute terms. We are calculating its value as implied by the price and volatility of the underlying and the risk-free rate. The probabilities of up and down movements are already incorporated in these prices and we don't need to take them into account again when pricing the option based on the stock. All of our methods of valuing derivatives share this approach. Investors' expected returns for underlyings are irrelevant in this calculation. All we are saying is that assuming the price for the underlying is known, then the binomial model can tell us the only fair price for the option—any other price would allow for arbitrage opportunities between the price of the underlying and the derivative.

This valuation method involves using "no-arbitrage arguments" and is also known as the Portfolio Approach or Delta Approach to valuing derivatives.

What is the Risk-Neutral Binomial Tree Method?

The concept of a portfolio made up of some portion of stock and some portion of a derivative on that stock gives rise to the ability to generate equivalent cash flows at end nodes of binomial trees, and this certainty of cash flows allows us to discount the cash flows at the risk-free rate. The ability to discount cash flows in the future at a known risk-free rate gives us the concept of *risk-neutral valuation*. Risk neutral valuation is a powerful concept in derivatives pricing which enables valuation of assets based on their expected payoffs at different points in time and with different scenarios of underlying asset price movements.

Risk-neutral valuation is applicable whenever you can create a portfolio including the underlying plus a derivative on the same underlying. It cannot be extrapolated to find the value of derivatives on other underlyings. It relies on the portfolio instruments having a level of dependency on one another.

This model is very flexible and powerful because we don't need to know the real probability of the upside scenario, or the real likelihood of the downside economic scenario—it is not required to maintain our certainty of cash flows at the end point.

An easy mistake to make is to confuse this constructed probability distribution with real-world probability. They will be different, but the method of risk-neutral pricing is, like many other useful computational tools, convenient and powerful. The approach of risk-neutral valuation makes sense for valuation purposes but only works when all of the instruments included in the valuation model depend on the same underlying and thus are exposed to the same risks, though held in different proportions. We are pricing the option in terms of the underlying stock, thus risk preferences are taken into account in the pricing of the underlying.

The risk-neutral binomial tree approach is mathematically equivalent to the portfolio approach previously covered, and gives us the exact same valuation. The risk neutral binomial tree valuation approach to value the derivative, *f*, is as follows.

$$f = e^{(-rT)}[p \cdot f_u + (1 - p) \cdot f_d]$$

Where

$$p = \frac{(e^{(rT)} - d)}{(u - d)}$$

d = (1 + the percentage move of the stock to reach the downside scenario price), and u = (1+ the percentage move of the stock to achieve the upside scenario price)

T = time to maturity measured in years or fractions of years

r = the risk-free rate

With some algebra, you can show that the risk-neutral formula is mathematically equivalent to the portfolio approach where Δ of shares is calculated to generate riskless outcomes at maturity, T.

Although we are not making any assumptions about the probabilities of the returns on the underlying, the element p in this formula can be interpreted as the "risk-neutral probability of an up move" and 1–p as the "risk-neutral probability of a down move."

The value today of the derivative, *f*, can thus be read as the present value of the derivative at the up node times the risk-neutral probability of an up move plus the value of the derivative at the down node times the risk-neutral probability of a down move (see Figure 6.3).

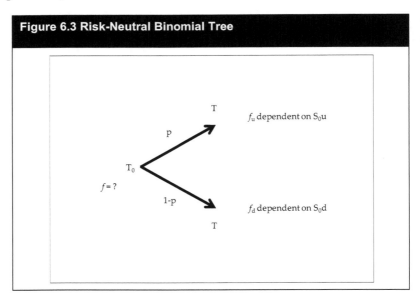

Figure 6.3 Risk-Neutral Binomial Tree

In our prior example of an underlying that has a price of $50, where we know at the end of three months that the underlying will be at one of two prices (either $70 or $30), we will price a European Call with a strike of $50, and one month to expiration and a risk-free interest rate of 5%.

Here p = 0.5052 based on the above formula where p is a function of the risk free rate and time to maturity T, as well as u and d. Then the call value at time zero is $f = e^{(-rT)}x[pf_u] = \$10.0624$, the same as in the portfolio valuation approach above.

How Do We Make This More Realistic?

You might agree with everything we have covered so far, but worry that we are relying on too many assumptions and are describing a world that is quite distant from real life. A world in which there are only two possible stock price outcomes over a one month period seems quite far from reality. Now that we have established some reasonable approaches for valuing a derivative in terms of the price of its underlying, we can begin to make the approach more and more like the real world of securities price movements. The first step in doing this is to extend the analysis to shorter and shorter time frames.

Multi-Step Binomial Trees

The ideas we developed for a single-period binomial model also apply to a multi-period approach. Next we will look at a two-step, or two time-period binomial tree. In this framework the stock price must follow one of four patterns (see Figure 6.4). For the two periods, the stock can go up-up, up-down, down-up, or down-down. At the moment, we are assuming fixed down and up percentages, the down-up and up-down paths will end with the same final stock price (but you will later see that this restriction is not required, the valuation approach is more flexible than this).

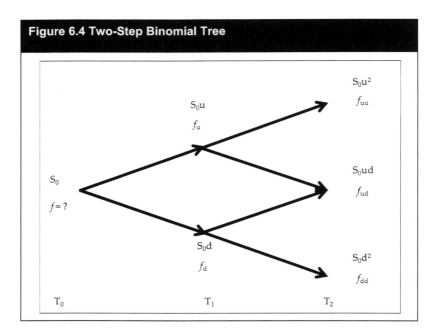

Figure 6.4 Two-Step Binomial Tree

The two step binomial tree can be expressed formulaically as well, as follows.

$$f_{u} = e^{-r(T_2 - T_1)}[p \cdot f_{uu} + (1 - p) \cdot f_{du}]$$

$$f_{d} = e^{-r(T_2 - T_1)}[p \cdot f_{du} + (1 - p) \cdot f_{dd}]$$

where
$$p = \frac{(e^{(r(T_2 - T_1))} - d)}{(u - d)}$$
then

$$f = e^{-r(T_1 - T_0)}[p \cdot f_{u} + (1 - p) \cdot f_{d}]$$

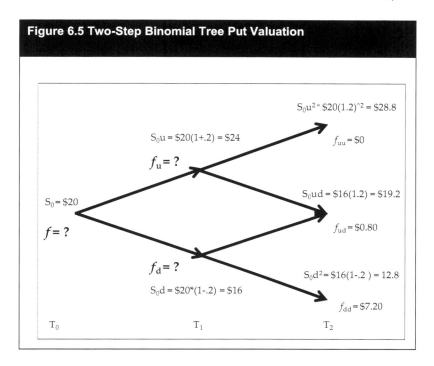

Figure 6.5 Two-Step Binomial Tree Put Valuation

$S_0 = \$20$

$f = ?$

$S_0u = \$20(1+.2) = \$24$

$f_u = ?$

$f_d = ?$

$S_0d = \$20*(1-.2) = \$16$

$S_0u^2 = \$20(1.2)^2 = \$28.8$

$f_{uu} = \$0$

$S_0ud = \$16(1.2) = \$19.2$

$f_{ud} = \$0.80$

$S_0d^2 = \$16(1-.2) = 12.8$

$f_{dd} = \$7.20$

T_0 T_1 T_2

Binomial trees can be used for valuing puts or calls. Consider a two step binomial tree, with each step one year long where at each node the stock moves up or down 20% and the risk-free rate is 5%. Suppose the stock price is now $20 and that we will try to value a put with a strike of $20 (see Figure 6.5).

You work from right to left, backward in time, valuing the option node by node, first calculating f_u and f_d using the above formulas, then value *f* using the formula:

$$f = e^{-r(T_1 - T_0)} [p \cdot f_u + (1 - p) \cdot f_d]$$

The first step is to calculate p using this formula:

$$p = \frac{(e^{(r(T_2 - T_1))} - d)}{(u - d)}$$

$p = [(e^{(0.05 \times 1)} - 0.8]/(1.2 - 0.8) = 0.6282$

$f_u = e^{(-rT)}[(1-p) \times 0.80] = \$0.28$

$f_d = e^{(-rT)}[p \times (0.80) + (1-p) \times (7.20)] = \$3.02$

$f = e^{(-rT)}[p \times 0.28 + (1-p) \times 3.02] = \$1.24$

Now that we have looked at a two-period binomial tree, you can easily see that we can, using the same formulas, produce binomial trees with as many nodes as we want. The more periods that we add, the more realistic our model becomes. A binomial tree with just 20 periods gives more than a million stock price movement patterns.

Clearly working out a series of one-second node one-penny price movement binomial trees would take quite a while, but it is easy to code the approach on your computer, and it is virtually unlimited as to how many nodes you can add. The binomial model assumes that movements in the price follow a binomial distribution. If you increase the number of nodes, and are modeling the stock price evolution over a very short period of time, you begin to approach a very realistic share price trajectory. Each node could be one second in duration, and show the stock's expected price moves of, as an example, up one penny or down one penny. This begins to approximate real-life stock price movements quite accurately.

At each second during a trading day, it is fairly realistic to assume that a $20 stock will increase or decrease by as little as $0.01 or $0.02. As you increase the number of nodes, this binomial distribution approaches the lognormal distribution assumed by Black–Scholes (see Chapter 7). When analyzed as a numerical procedure, the Cox, Ross, and Rubinstein binomial method can be viewed as a special case of the explicit finite difference method for the Black-Scholes partial differential equation.

The binomial tree approach is very flexible, and can take into account dividends, early exercise opportunities, and even different distributions of stock price movements over the time to maturity of the derivative being valued. This means that you could model low volatility periods of stock price movements, and then higher volatility periods for the stock—perhaps around their earnings announcements—over the duration of an option's life.

Although computationally slower than the Black–Scholes formula, it is more accurate, particularly for longer-dated options on securities with dividend payments. For these reasons, various versions of the binomial model are widely used by practitioners in the options markets. For options with several sources of uncertainty and for options with complicated features, binomial methods can be less practical due to several difficulties, at which point Monte Carlo option models are used instead (see Chapter 13).

Pricing American Options

American options can be exercised anytime up to maturity, as opposed to European options which can only be exercised at maturity. Binomial trees can be used to price American options with the only modification needed is to evaluate at each node as to whether there is more value associated with exercising or holding the option to expiration. The highest of these two values is used in calculating the option value.

In the two-step American binomial tree valuation shown in Figure 6.6, we have the earlier put example, with the option now American. In this case, at T_1 it would be optimal to early-exercise. Thus the valuation at the first down node is in fact the early-exercise valuation, which is the intrinsic value at that node, as opposed to the valuation achieved from the risk-neutral valuation for f_d. At time zero, the valuation of the derivative is based on f_u as usual, but the f_d value input into the formula for f is the early exercise cash flow.

Figure 6.6 Two-Step American Put Valuation

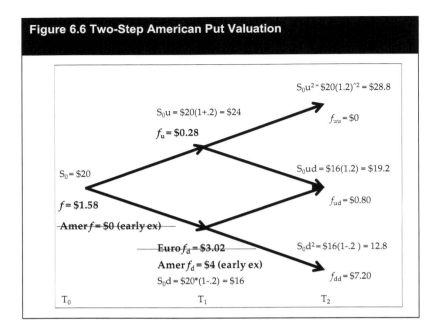

$S_0u^2 = \$20(1.2)^{\wedge}2 = \$28.8$

$f_{uu} = \$0$

$S_0u = \$20(1+.2) = \$24$

$f_u = \$0.28$

$S_0 = \$20$

$S_0ud = \$16(1.2) = \$19.2$

$f = \$1.58$

$f_{ud} = \$0.80$

~~Amer $f = \$0$ (early ex)~~

~~Euro $f_d = \$3.02$~~

$S_0d^2 = \$16(1-.2) = 12.8$

Amer $f_d = \$4$ (early ex)

$S_0d = \$20*(1-.2) = \$16$

$f_{dd} = \$7.20$

T_0 T_1 T_2

When Should You Exercise an American Option?

In most cases, options should not be exercised before expiration because doing so is value destructive. This is because the value of an option at a given point in time is made up of both its intrinsic value (the value available from exercising early) and its time value. Selling an option rather than early-exercising it will almost always be more profitable due to the time value component.

For an American-style call option, early exercise makes sense whenever the benefits of being long the underlying outweighs the cost of giving up the option early (the benefits of being long the underlying outweigh the foregone time value of the option). For example, on the day before an ex-dividend date, it may make sense to exercise an equity call option early in order to collect the dividend. In general, equity call options should only be exercised early on the day before an ex-dividend date, and then only for deep in-the-money options when the dividend is sufficiently large (see Figure 6.7).

Figure 6.7 illustrates a scenario where a dividend of $2.50 per share is expected to be paid immediately prior to expiration of an option. Call option holders, though holding "bullish" or "long" positions with respect to the underlying asset, are not eligible to collect dividends paid on the underlyings. Therefore, if a long American call option holder expects at T_0 and at T_1 that a dividend will be paid on the underlying stock just prior to the option's maturity at T_2, they can evaluate whether or not it is optimal to early-exercise. Analysizing potential early exercise at T_0 shows there is no benefit to early exercising since the option is not in-the-money. At T_1, the up node is in-the-money, the American call holder evaluates if holding or early-exercising is optimal. Early-exercising has a value at T_1 in the up node of $3.00 ($30 share price less $30 strike). Using the European options binomial tree pricing formula fu in the up node, the call option is valued at only $2.73. This valuation difference came about because the expected value of the spot at T_2 is reduced by $2.50 just prior to expiration. This dividend payment is of sufficient size, in this case (it is not always optimal to early-exercise on dividend-paying stocks, prior to expiration, it depends on the relative size of the dividend), that the underlying asset's price drop due to the dividend payment makes early-exercise the optimal strategy.

For an American-style put option, early exercise might make sense if it is deep in-the-money. In this case, it may be wise to exercise the option early in order to obtain the intrinsic value $(K - S)$ earlier so that it can start to earn interest immediately. This is somewhat more likely to be worthwhile if there is no ex-dividend date, which would probably cause the price of the underlying to fall further between now and the expiry date. This would usually require interest rates to be relatively high.

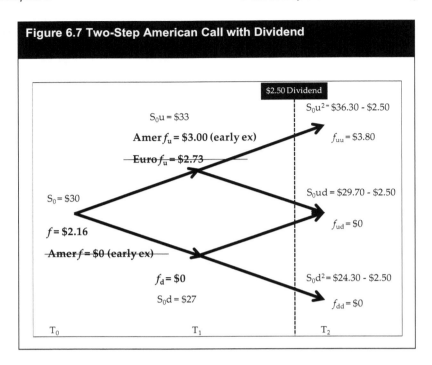

Figure 6.7 Two-Step American Call with Dividend

Figure 6.7 is an example of an American call option, where the company is expected to pay a dividend just prior to the option exercise date. The current stock price is $30, the call strike is $30, the risk-free interest rate is 5%, the option expires in 2 years and the stock is paying a dividend of $2.50 one day prior to the option's expiration. The shares are expected to rise or fall 10% each year.

Asset Volatility in Binomial Tree Valuation

The volatility of the underlying asset has not yet been discussed, and how it relates to the Binomial Tree Options Pricing Model. However, it is implicitly a very important driver of the model and its subsequent outputs. The sizes of the upward and downward movements at each node, u and d, relate directly to the volatility of the underlying and time elapsed between nodes.

$$u = e^{\sigma\sqrt{(T_1-T_0)}} \qquad\qquad \text{and} \qquad\qquad d = \frac{1}{u}$$

Thus, given an underlying's price, volatility, and the risk-free interest rate, you should be able to construct a binomial tree and price any option on that underlying.

Chapter 6 Questions

1. Does pricing an option using the binomial tree approach give you a perfect price for an option? Do all options trade at exactly the prices that you would expect if you priced them using this method? Explain the reasoning behind your answer.

2. If a stock followed the path of a two-step binomial tree, with the same u and d for each of the two time periods, what is the chance that the stock price will be unchanged at the end of the two periods?

3. A stock is currently trading at $40. Suppose we know that in two months it will be either $43 or $38, and we know that the risk-free rate is 5% with continuous compounding. What is the value of a two-month European call option with a strike of $39? Use no-arbitrage arguments or the "portfolio approach" to valuing the option.

4. Calculate the value of a European put using a binomial tree on a stock trading now at $40 where we know that at the end of three months it will be either $45 or $35, the risk-free rate is 6% quarterly compounded and the strike is $40.

5. Explain why the binomial tree approach to pricing options requires a portfolio approach?

6. Calculate the value of a European call option using a two-step binomial tree. Each step in the tree is a three month period. The stock will either go up by 6% or down by 5% at each period. The risk-free rate is 5% per year continuously compounded, and the strike is $51.

7. Why is the binomial tree so named? What is binomial about it?

8. Calculate the values of u, d, and p for use in a binomial tree to price a foreign exchange option. The tree step size is three months. The foreign interest rate is 8% per annum, the domestic

interest rate is 5% per annum, and the volatility is 12% per annum.

9. Explain the idea of risk-neutral valuation.

10. A stock is trading at $100 and in the next year it will either rise by 10% or fall by 20%. The risk-free rate is 4%. A call option on this stock has a strike price of $105 and expires in one year. What is the chance that the stock price will rise in the next year? What is the price of the call option?

11. Based on the information in the last question, what would the price of the option be if it expired in two years and it could move up by 10% per year or down 20% per year?

12. XYZ stock is a non-dividend paying stock trading at $198. Calculate the price of a nine-month $200 XYZ call option if the risk-free rate is 8% per annum and the volatility is 30% per annum. Use a binomial tree with a time step of three months to answer this question.

13. Calculate the answer to the last question using a binomial tree with a time step of one year. Is the answer the same? Explain.

14. Using a two-step binomial tree, calculate the value of an American call option where the underlying stock pays a dividend of $1 per share just before the option's expiration. The stock is trading at $22, the strike is $20, the risk-free rate is 4%. The option is outstanding for another two years (each step in the binomial tree is one year long). The stock is expected to rise or fall 10% in each one-year period prior to expiry.

Chapter 7

THE BLACK-SCHOLES PRICING METHOD

The *Black-Scholes Model* is probably the best known and most widely used model for option pricing. The model was first published by Fischer Black and Myron Scholes in their 1973 paper, "The Pricing of Options and Corporate Liabilities," published in the *Journal of Political Economy*. In the paper, they derived a partial differential equation, now called the Black-Scholes equation, which estimates the price of an option over time. The key idea behind the model was that you could follow a trading strategy in an underlying instrument which would perfectly hedge your exposure to the price swings in the option, and, as a consequence, eliminate risk. This type of hedging is known as *dynamic hedging*.

Robert C. Merton was the first to publish a paper expanding the mathematical understanding of the options pricing model, and coined the term "Black-Scholes options pricing model." Merton and Scholes received the 1997 Nobel Memorial Prize in Economic Sciences for their work. Though ineligible for the prize because of his death in 1995, Black was mentioned as a contributor by the Swedish Academy.

While the Black-Scholes formula is quite specific in its assumptions, the method of deriving the Black-Scholes partial differential equation (PDE) is quite general. The model's assumptions have been relaxed and generalized in many directions, leading to numerous models that are currently used in derivative pricing and risk management. Both the model and the insights of the model such as no-arbitrage bounds and risk-neutral pricing are widely used in practice.

The Black-Scholes formula has only one parameter that cannot be observed in the market: the average future volatility of the underlying asset.

Model Assumptions

There are a number of assumptions that the Black-Scholes model relies upon. The most important one is that underlying asset prices follow a geometric Brownian Motion. This means that asset prices must be lognormally distributed and that asset prices must be continuous and cannot "jump."

The full list of assumptions are as follows:

1. The stock price follows a geometric Brownian motion with a constant μ (expected return) and σ volatility.

2. Securities can be sold short, and the proceeds can be used in full.

3. There are no taxes or trading costs. All securities are perfectly divisible.

4. There are no dividends on the underlying over the life of the option.

5. There are no arbitrage opportunities available in markets.

6. Trading is continuous (no overnight market closures).

7. Borrowing and lending occurs at the same rate, r, is a constant.

Stock prices are assumed to follow a stochastic (random pattern) process, the most commonly used model of stock price behavior is:

$$\frac{dS}{S} = \mu\, dt + \sigma\, dW$$

The variable σ is the volatility of the stock price, μ is the expected rate of return, and W is a stochastic (random) variable (Brownian motion). Note that W represents the only source of uncertainty in the price history of the stock. Intuitively, W(t) is a process that moves up and down in a random manner such that its expected change over any time interval is 0.

Are these Assumptions Reasonable?

The assumptions of continuous changes in asset prices and continuous trading are clearly imperfect but form a decent approximation of reality for many markets. Most liquid, publicly traded equities traded on major exchanges show nearly continuous price movements throughout their trading days and, in some cases, trade in a nearly 24-hour cycle. When primary exchanges are closed, many stocks trade in "overnight" sessions. These may be less liquid than on their formal trading day and on their primary exchange, but they still provide investors access to enter and exit trades and for price discovery on a nearly 24-hour basis.

Unlike the Black-Scholes assumption that stock prices should never gap, we do regularly observe that prices "gap." The price formation and news arrival processes are inherently discrete, not continuous. Prices often experience "jumps." The assumption of constant volatility of returns is thus also unrealistic and is violated in practice. Many events can cause stocks to experience temporary or longer-lasting volatility shifts, including: earnings surprises; major corporate action announcements such as mergers, stock splits, or special dividends; accusations of fraud; regulatory violations; being hacked; or business-altering research results (FDA drug approval or successfully launching a self-driving car).

The assumption of constant interest rates is also unrealistic and violated in practice. In reality, market interest rates, and risk-free rates move around with investors' risk appetites and with the movements of central banks around the world.

Black-Scholes Model Notation

S_0 = spot price of underlying at time zero

f = options value

c = European call

p = European put

K = strike price

e = Euler's number, the base of the natural logarithm 2.71828

r = the risk-free rate

σ = the standard deviation of a stock's returns

T = time in years, we generally use now = 0, expiry = T

Π = the value of a portfolio

$N(x)$ = the standard normal cumulative distribution function,

$$N(x) = \frac{1}{\sqrt{2\pi}} \int_{-\infty}^{x} e^{-\frac{z^2}{2}} \, dz$$

$N'_{(x)}$ = the standard normal probability density function

$$N'(x) = \frac{1}{\sqrt{2\pi}} e^{-\frac{x^2}{2}}$$

The Black-Scholes Model Equation

The Black-Scholes equation is a partial differential equation (PDE)—an equation involving functions and their partial derivatives—describing the price evolution of a European call or European put under the Black–Scholes model over time. The equation is:

$$\frac{\partial V}{\partial t} + \frac{1}{2}\sigma^2 S^2 \frac{\partial^2 V}{\partial S^2} + rS\frac{\partial V}{\partial S} - rV = 0$$

The key insight behind the equation is that one can perfectly hedge the option by dynamically hedging and consequently have a risk-free portfolio of the underlying and the option over time. The existence of this trading strategy implies that there is only one right price for the option, as returned by the Black-Scholes formula.

The Black-Scholes Formula

The Black-Scholes formula calculates the price of European put and call options. This formula can be obtained by solving the equation for the corresponding terminal and boundary conditions.

The value of a call option for a non-dividend-paying underlying stock in terms of the Black–Scholes parameters is:

$$C(S,t) = N(d_1)S - N(d_2)Ke^{-r(T-t)}$$
$$d_1 = \frac{1}{\sigma\sqrt{T-t}}\left[\ln\left(\frac{S}{K}\right) + \left(r + \frac{\sigma^2}{2}\right)(T-t)\right]$$
$$d_2 = \frac{1}{\sigma\sqrt{T-t}}\left[\ln\left(\frac{S}{K}\right) + \left(r - \frac{\sigma^2}{2}\right)(T-t)\right]$$
$$= d_1 - \sigma\sqrt{T-t}$$

The price of a corresponding put option due to put-call parity is:

$$P(S,t) = Ke^{-r(T-t)} - S + C(S,t)$$
$$= N(-d_2)Ke^{-r(T-t)} - N(-d_1)S$$

N(x) is the cumulative distribution function of the standard normal distribution, the function for this in Microsoft Excel is =NORMDIST(). T – where t is the time to maturity.

Black-Scholes Model Interpretations

The Black-Scholes model can be interpreted as calculating the weighted probabilities and values of various share price outcomes versus the strikes. The model tells us that we can perfectly price European-style options as long as the underlying asset moves in a Brownian Motion-like manner, which means: It moves with a certain drift or expected return μ and with a stationary volatility σ. In practice, this is not a perfect explanation of stock price movements, but it is a good proxy. Like any model, it is a simplification of an extremely complex system. The model is still good enough to be extensively used and most more-recent models tend to be small modifications on the basic Black-Scholes model.

Black-Scholes Model Inputs

The Black-Scholes model for the price of an option depends on five variables:

1. The stock price

2. The exercise price

3. The time until expiration

4. The risk-free rate

5. The standard deviation of the stock

All of these variables can be known with certainty with the exception of the last two.

Black-Scholes and the Risk-Free Rate

The Black-Scholes model requires a risk-free rate, and we can use the US Treasury bill rate as a good proxy for this. If the yield curve has a steep slope, yields can be quite different for different maturities. Treasury bills mature every week and the correct bill to use is the one that matures closest to the option expiration. You can average the bid and offered yields to estimate the true yield which lies between the two.

Volatility and Black-Scholes

Estimating the standard deviation is more difficult and more important than estimating the risk-free rate. The Black-Scholes model assumes that you know the average future volatility of the stock, and that this volatility is constant over the life of the option. There are two basic ways of estimating the volatility. The first involves analyzing historic data to calculate the standard deviation, the second uses live option prices to back out the market's estimate of standard deviation. This is known as *implied volatility*.

Historic Volatility and Black-Scholes

We can take some historic stock price data and calculate its standard deviation to come up with an estimate of the volatility of the underlying in the past. While this is useful, it is not going to give you a perfect price for an option. If one person uses one month of historical data, another person uses six months of data, and a third person used a year's worth of price data, they would all come up with different volatilities, and thus different option prices. On top of this, the volatility we need for the formula is the future *realized volatility*, which is unknowable. Another problem associated with using historic data is that apart from economic conditions changing over time, companies also change over time. A company might have just issued a huge amount of debt in the last week, and thus its expected volatility over the next six months may be significantly different than over the last six months. The company might also have launched new products, entered new business areas, or have bought another company recently, all of which would be expected to affect its volatility, all other things being kept equal.

In using historic data for the Black-Scholes formula you must match the unit of time used to that used in the interest rate and the time to expiration. If you calculate a daily standard deviation, you can convert it into a comparable yearly estimate. Because markets are not open on weekends and holidays, there are roughly 250 trading days in a year, not 365. We have already seen that stock prices are distributed with a standard deviation that increases as the square root of time. Thus we can adjust the time component of our standard deviation estimate by multiplying it by the square root of time.

$$\text{Annualized } \sigma = \text{Daily } \sigma \times \sqrt{250}$$

There are arguments to be made for using various lengths of time data. Some would argue for using only 10 days, which would emphasize very recent swings, while others would use quite a long series. Statisticians would argue that we always get a more reliable estimate by using a longer series. There is no correct answer to this, and we face a trade-off between using the most data and using the most current data.

Implied Volatility

Implied volatility is a forward-looking expectation of volatility of the price of the underlying security. It differs from *historical volatility* in that it is not calculated from known past returns of a security. The implied volatility of an option contract is the value of the volatility of the underlying instrument which is backed out from an options pricing model by inputting all of the known inputs and the market price of the option and solving for volatility. Implied volatility is backed out from real live option prices. Implied volatility tells us what the market believes future volatility will be like on an underlying until the option's maturity. It is a sum of all market participants' best guesses as to how risky an asset will be in the future.

Implied volatility is such an important feature of options markets that many options are quoted on implied volatility alone as opposed to the premium price. The implied volatility is a more useful measure than its price to professional options traders of the option's relative value.

Volatility is usually the key feature being traded in the options space. Options professionals are primarily placing bets on the pricing of the implied volatility of the underlying as opposed to the direction of the underlying. For this reason, within banks and hedge funds options traders are usually referred to as volatility traders.

Volatility Indices

Volatility indices are indices that track the value of implied volatility of other derivative securities. For instance, the CBOE Volatility Index (VIX) is calculated from a weighted average of implied volatilities of various options on the S&P500 Index (see Figure 7.1). There are also other well known volatility indices such as: the VXN index; the Nasdaq 100 Index futures volatility measure; the QQV, QQQ Nasdaq ETF volatility measure; IVX—Implied Volatility Index, an expected stock volatility over a future period for any of US securities and exchange traded instruments; as well as options and futures that are tradable based upon on these volatility indices. The increased liquidity of these markets in recent years has meant that prices of the VIX futures are being used to price S&P options, creating a circular reference within these market instruments.

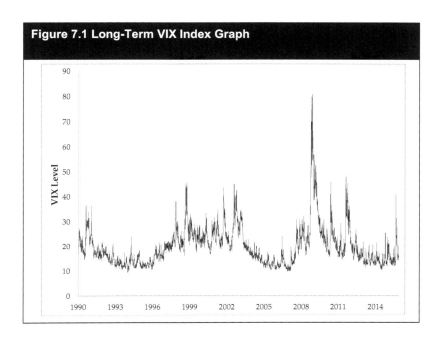

Figure 7.1 Long-Term VIX Index Graph

European Options and Dividends

The Black-Scholes model assumes that the underlying stock pays no dividends, but most of the stocks that options are traded on are dividend paying stocks. In fact 85% of the stocks in the S&P500 pay dividends. While the Black-Scholes model was a great breakthrough in financial mathematics, solving the problem of pricing options on dividend paying stocks was of great importance.

Dividends that are paid out over the life of a stock option can be expected to impact the stock price and thus should affect the pricing of the option. For most stocks, the dividend payments likely to occur during the life of an option can be projected with reasonable accuracy. All other things being equal, an investor would expect a $1 dividend to cause the price of the stock to fall by $1 ex dividend. In practice, because of taxes, the stock price might be expected to fall by slightly less than the amount of the dividend, and in this case you would use the present value of the expected stock price drop instead of the amount of the dividend. To build an expected dividend into the Black-Scholes model we can subtract the present value of an expected dividend from the current stock price and then apply the Black-Scholes model as usual but using this adjusted stock price as a starting point.

Merton's Model

Robert Merton built a model that allows us to account for dividends that are paid out at a continuous rate. The adjustment for continuous dividends treats the dividend rate as a negative interest rate. We let q represent this continuous dividend.

Then we use Merton's Model, which is simply a modified Black-Scholes model to price options.

$$C(S_0, t) = e^{-r(T-t)}[FN(d_1) - KN(d_2)]$$

and

$$P(S_0, t) = e^{-r(T-t)}[KN(-d_2) - FN(-d_1)]$$

where the modified forward price occurring in the terms d_1, d_2 is

$$F = S_0 e^{(r-q)(T-t)}$$

$$d_1 = \frac{1}{\sigma\sqrt{T-t}}\left[\ln\left(\frac{S_0}{K}\right) + (r - q + \frac{1}{2}\sigma^2)(T-t)\right]$$

and

$$d_2 = d_1 - \sigma\sqrt{T-t}$$

American Options and Black-Scholes

Because American options can be exercised at any time before the expiration date, they must trade at some premium to an otherwise identical European option. The problem in pricing an American option relates to the problem of finding the optimal time to exercise the option. The value of the right of early exercise is known as the "early exercise premium." The work in pricing American options relates to valuing the early exercise premium. In general there is no closed form solution for pricing American options.

The difference in prices between American and European options depends largely upon the "moneyness" of the option, the interest rate, the amount of time left until expiry, and whether the underlying pays dividends.

For an American call option, early exercise is reasonable whenever the benefit of being long the underlying outweighs the cost of giving up the option early. For example, on the day before an ex-dividend date, it may make sense to exercise an equity call option early in order to collect the dividend. In general, equity call options should only be exercised early on the day before an ex-dividend date, and then only for deep in-the-money options. If a stock is non dividend paying, calls should have no early exercise premium.

For an American put option, early exercise is reasonable for deep in-the-money options. In this case, it may make sense to exercise the option early in order to obtain the intrinsic value $(K - S)$ earlier so that it can start to earn interest immediately. This is somewhat more likely to be worthwhile if there is no ex-dividend date between now and the expiration date. It usually requires a high interest rate environment.

Fischer Black's approach to pricing American call options followed these steps.

1. Subtract the present value of all expected dividends over the life of the option from the current stock price.
2. For each dividend date, reduce the exercise price by the present value of all dividends yet to be paid, including the dividend that is about to be paid.

3. Taking each dividend date and the actual expiration date of the option as possible expiration dates, compute the value of a European call using the adjusted stock and exercise prices.
4. Select the highest of these European call values as the estimate of the value of the American call.

This approach takes into account that it is only ever optimal to early exercise a call option just prior to a dividend payment and analyzes a American call as a series of European calls each expiring just before each dividend payment and at the actual expiration date.

Valuing American put options using the Black-Scholes model is more difficult. Barone-Adesi and Whaley developed an approximation formula for pricing American options. In their approach, the stochastic differential equation is split into two components: the European option value and the early exercise premium. With some assumptions, a quadratic equation that approximates the solution for the early exercise premium is then obtained. This solution involves finding the critical value, s*, such that an investor is indifferent between early exercise and holding to maturity.

Bjerksund and Stensland provide an approximation based on an exercise strategy corresponding to a trigger price. Here, if the underlying asset price is greater than or equal to the trigger price it is optimal to exercise, and the value must equal $S - K$, otherwise the option can be reduced to a combination of a European up-and-out call option (which is a type of "exotic" option, discussed in a later Chapter, where, if the underlying rises above a given knock-out price during the life of the option, the call option expires worthless) and a rebate that is received at the knock-out date if the option is knocked out prior to the maturity date. The formula can then be modified for the valuation of a put option, using put-call parity.

Chapter 7 Questions

1. Which parameter of the Black-Scholes model cannot be observed in the market?

2. Is the Black-Scholes model superior to the Binomial Tree approach in pricing all options? Explain.

3. List the seven assumptions underlying the Black-Scholes model.

4. Discuss how reasonable each of the seven assumptions underlying the Black Scholes model are.

5. What are the five variables required to calculate the Black-Scholes price of an option?

6. What interest rate do we use in the Black-Scholes model, and why?

7. How do you come up with a volatility figure to use in pricing options using the Black-Scholes formula? Explain.

8. Take the following sequence of daily closing stock prices: $25, $27, $26, $24, $26, $28, $29. Calculate the mean daily logarithmic return, the daily standard deviation of returns, and the annualized standard deviation of returns. Show your calculations.

9. Explain the difference between implied volatility, historic volatility, and realized volatility.

10. How can the Black-Scholes formula be adjusted to price an option on a dividend-paying stock?

11. Is it ever optimal to early exercise an American option? Explain.

12. Explain the steps in Fischer Black's approach to pricing American call options.

13. Can the Black-Scholes formula be used to price American put options?

14. XYZ stock is trading at $100, and has a volatility of 40%. The risk-free rate is 4%. Use the Black-Scholes formula to price an at-the-money European call option, and an at-the-money European put option, each of which expires in half a year.

15. Taking the information from the last problem, assume that the stock pays a dividend of $2 in three months (1/4 of a year). Apply a dividend adjustment to the Black-Scholes model and calculate new call and put prices.

Chapter 8

THE OPTIONS GREEKS

In the last chapter we explained that the price of a European option depends on the price of the underlying, the exercise price, the interest rate, the volatility of the underlying, and the time until expiration. Now we will look at the sensitivity of option prices to these factors and see how a knowledge of these influences can drive trading strategies and improve options trading techniques. How much will the movements in one or another of these factors change the valuation of an option?

What is Hedging?

Hedging refers to all trading activity that reduces risks, minimizes unwanted financial exposures or neutralizes portfolio risks. A "well-hedged trading book" is a portfolio that should experience very few gains or losses regardless of market movements.

When banks or financial institutions trade derivatives, they usually do some hedging. In particular, market makers or middlemen nearly always try to hedge away most of their exposures. They are usually just trying to earn profits from bid/offer spreads or commissions earned on a per-trade basis, as opposed to formulating views on the directions of assets, and carrying those risks over time.

The only perfect hedge for a given position is to trade the precisely equal and offsetting derivative so that you have no residual position. Often this is not possible, or would negate all of the gains earned from bid/offer spreads and commissions, and whenever you are hedging with a very similar, but not identical, financial instrument, you are usually left with some risk exposure.

The Options Greeks

"The Greeks" is the term in the options world for the measures of sensitivity of the price of a derivative to changes in individual parameter values while holding all other parameters fixed. They are partial derivatives of the options price with respect to the individual parameter values. Some Greeks such as gamma are partial derivatives of another Greek, "delta" in this case. They are referred to as "The Greeks" because the most common of these sensitivities are denoted by Greek letters. Collectively, these can also be called the "risk sensitivities" or "risk measures."

The Greeks are of great importance to active derivatives traders. The Greeks of a derivatives portfolio are crucial for understanding and risk-managing options-heavy portfolios. The Greeks tell a portfolio manager how the portfolio should behave in various market environments. Financial institutions will typically give a trader or trading desk risk limits based upon the portfolio Greeks that must not be exceeded.

The Greeks are all about change, they tell us how option prices change when one of the inputs to the pricing formula changes. Calculus is the mathematical study of change, and is used to derive the Greeks.

Delta Δ

Delta is the amount the options price changes for a one unit change in the price of the underlying. Mathematically speaking, it is the first derivative of the option price with respect to the underlying. It is typically expressed in terms of the amount an options position's value will change given a 1% move in the underlying share price. These estimates of the price change are only approximate.

$$\Delta = \frac{\partial V}{\partial S}$$

Delta can be understood as a ratio comparing the change in the price in the underlying asset (S) to the corresponding change in the price of the derivative (V). For example, if a call had a delta of 0.6, you would expect the call to rise by $0.60 for every $1 rise in the price of the underlying stock.

Delta is the slope of the tangent line to the option value. The delta of a vanilla call option can only range from 0 to 1. Delta will be low at low spot prices, and high at high spot prices, relative to the strike price.Figures 8.1 and 8.2 show call delta plotted as the tangent line to the option's value. Delta is a linear approximation of a curved function, and thus it accurately tracks options value changes only for small changes in the price of the underlying.

Relationship Between Put and Call Delta

Delta is always positive for long calls and negative for long puts; thus, the value of a call increases with a stock price increase, while the value of a put decreases if the stock price increases. Given a European call and put option for the same underlying, strike price, and time to maturity and with no dividend yield, the delta of the call minus the delta of the put equals 1. This is due to put-call parity: a long call plus a short put replicates a forward, which has delta equal to 1.

If the delta of a call is known to be 0.3 you can easily calculate the delta of the corresponding put at the same strike price as follows:

$$0.3 - 1 = -0.7$$

To calculate the delta of the corresponding call from the delta of a put, you can similarly add 1 to the put delta as follows:

$$-0.7 + 1 = 0.3$$

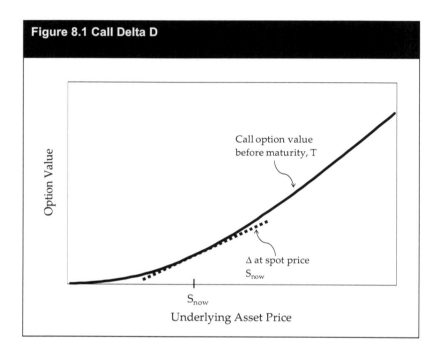

Figure 8.1 Call Delta D

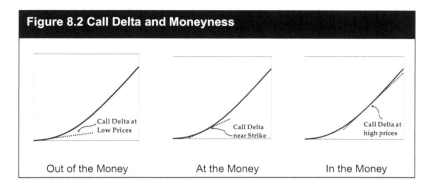

Figure 8.2 Call Delta and Moneyness

Call delta is always positive.

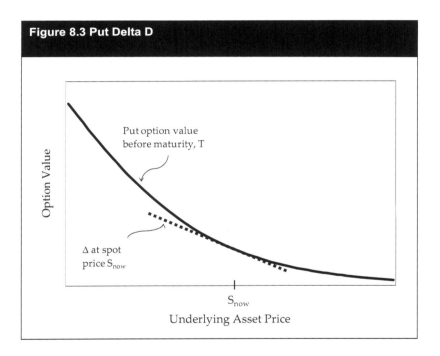

Figure 8.3 Put Delta D

Put delta is always negative.

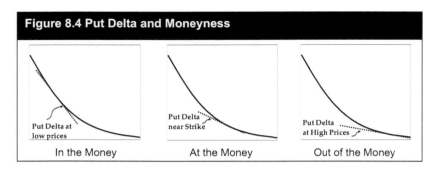

Figure 8.4 Put Delta and Moneyness

| In the Money | At the Money | Out of the Money |

The Intuition of Delta

Options values change in a non-linear manner, with a complicated formula for precise calculations. Delta is a quick way of determining at a given spot price how option values change for small movements in the price of the underlying over the next short period of time. Delta also tells you how long or short your portfolio is at a given point.

You can think of the delta of an option in terms of being long or short the underlying asset. If you are long one at-the-money call with a delta of 0.5, it is economically similar to being long 50 shares of the stock (with stock options, each call covers 100 shares).

Traders usually refer to a 0.6 delta call as a *60 delta call*, presenting the delta as a percentage of the total number of shares represented by the option contract. This is useful as the option will, for small price changes, behave like the number of shares indicated by the delta. For example, if a portfolio of 100 American call options on ABC each have a delta of 0.3 (=30%), it will gain or lose value just like 30 shares of ABC as the stock experiences small price movements.

The total delta of a portfolio of options on the same underlying asset can be calculated by simply taking the sum of the deltas for each individual position. Since the delta of underlying asset is always 1.0, a trader could delta-hedge the entire position in the underlying by buying or shorting the number of shares indicated by the total portfolio delta. This hedge will work for small movements in the price of the underlying, for a short amount of time, and notwithstanding changes in other market conditions such as volatility and the risk-free rate.

Delta-Neutral Portfolios

A *delta-neutral* portfolio is a portfolio made up of positions with offsetting positive and negative deltas so that the net delta is zero. Such a portfolio typically contains options and their corresponding underlying securities so that positive and negative delta components offset each other. In a delta-neutral portfolio you would expect the portfolio's value to be reasonably insensitive to changes in the value of the underlying security. The existence of a delta-neutral portfolio was shown as part of the original proof of the Black-Scholes model.

Theta θ

Theta measures the sensitivity of option values to the passage of time. The tendency for options premium prices to fall due to the passage of time is also known as *time decay*. Theta is the first derivative of the Black-Scholes option pricing model, with respect to time remaining to maturity.

Theta is intuitively easy to understand. Longer dated options are intuitively going to be worth more than shorter dated options, simply as the more time left until expiration, the more time an underlying has to make a big move and become deep in the money. Long options holders hope that the underlying will move dramatically; more time allows for more drama. Long options positions are usually worth less every day (see Figure 8.5).

The formula for Theta is:
$$\Theta = -\frac{\partial V}{\partial \tau}$$

The result of the above formula, the change in the option's value over time, gives us theta per year, usually we divide the result by the number of days in a year, with trading days in a year usually estimated to be 250 or 252, to arrive at the amount of money per share of the underlying that the option loses in one day.

Theta is almost always negative for long calls and puts and positive for short (or written) calls and puts, there are however some exceptions[5]. The total theta for a portfolio of options can be determined by summing the thetas for each individual position.

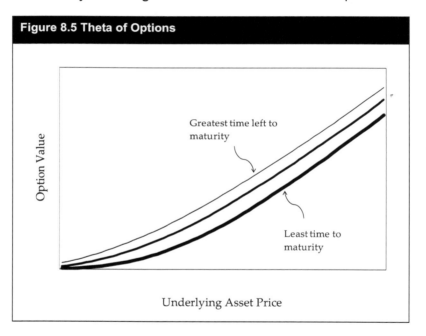

Figure 8.5 Theta of Options

Greatest time left to maturity

Least time to maturity

Option Value

Underlying Asset Price

Theta is a little different from our other Greeks. You can hedge against delta, gamma, rho, and vega, but you cannot hedge against time. It is not uncertain, you know it is going to happen. Despite this

---

[5] Exceptions are rare: applies for deep in the money European put options on stocks that don't pay dividends, or deep in the money European call options where there is a very high interest rate.

fact, many traders consider theta to be useful as it can be a proxy for gamma (described in the Gamma section below) within a delta-neutral portfolio.

When gamma is positive and large, theta is negative and large. With positive gamma, changes in the underlying result in higher option values. When there are no changes in the underlying price, the option value declines as expiration approaches, here theta is negative. When gamma is negative and large, changes in stock prices result in lower option values—thus when there is no stock price change, the value of the option increases as you approach expiration, and theta is positive.

Rho ρ

Rho measures the sensitivity of options prices to changes in interest rates. It is the first derivative of the option value with respect to the risk-free interest rate. Interest rates are a key input into options pricing formulas, and if they change, the options value will also change. Rho is typically expressed as how much options prices change (V) if the risk-free interest rate rises or falls by 1% per annum (r).

$$\rho = \frac{\partial V}{\partial r}$$

An increase in the risk-free rate increases call values and decreases put values. Rho is positive for long calls and negative for long puts.

Rho changes as time passes moving toward zero as expiration approaches. Rho tends to be low for a call option that is deep out of the money, and high for a deep in the money call. Rho tends to be high for a put option that is deep out of the money, and low for a deep in the money put.

Except under extreme circumstances, the value of an option is less sensitive to changes in the risk-free interest rate than to changes in other parameters. For this reason, rho is the least used of the first-order Greeks.

However, there is a dual effect to interest rate changes that the mathematical calculation of rho doesn't fully capture. An interest rate change typically will have two instant real-life impacts on the options price:

1.   from the rho as calculated above, the first derivative of the options price with respect to interest rate changes, and

2.   from the interest rate's impact on the underlying asset's price!

Risk-free rate movements cause equity prices to shift. An increase in a risk-free rate usually causes asset prices to decline, as they are being discounted at a higher rate; and conversely, a decline in the risk-free rate usually causes asset prices to rise as they are being discounted now at a lower rate. However, this effect is not captured in the calculation for rho. The calculation for rho is simply the first derivative of the Black-Scholes option price formula with respect to the interest rate factor, holding all other variables constant.

Vega ν

Vega measures the sensitivity of option prices (V) to changes in the volatility of the underlying. It is the first derivative of the Black-Scholes option price taken with respect to volatility σ.

$$\nu = \frac{\partial V}{\partial \sigma}$$

One of the core Black-Scholes assumptions is that σ stays constant over time. In practice σ does not stay constant. Vega analyzes how options values change when σ expectations change. Vega is typically expressed as the change in an option's value as volatility rises or falls by 1%. All long options positions, both calls and puts, will gain value with rising volatility.

Vega is not actually the name of a Greek letter, the name was possibly adopted because the Greek letter nu looks like the Latin letter v, and vega rhymes with the American pronunciation of beta and theta.

Positive vega means that an option's position increases in value when the underlying stock's volatility increases, and that the option's position decreases in value when the underlying stock's volatility decreases. It is often a little confusing at first that both puts and calls will increase in value with an increase in the underlying stocks volatility, but understanding this mechanism is probably the most important part of understanding how options work. This relationship is further explained in the chapter on dynamic hedging and volatility arbitrage.

Vega is one of the most important Greeks an options trader monitors, especially when markets are volatile. The prices of options can be particularly sensitive to changes in volatility especially in certain combinations such as straddles.

Gamma Γ

Gamma is a second-order Greek, it measures the sensitivity of delta to changes in the price of the underlying. It is the second derivative of the Black-Scholes option price taken with respect to the price of the underlying.

$$\Gamma = \frac{\partial \Delta}{\partial S} = \frac{\partial^2 V}{\partial S^2}$$

Gamma tells us how much delta should change for a 1% move in the price of the underlying. If Gamma is small, delta changes slowly and delta-neutral hedging is not as frequently required. If Gamma is large then delta is very sensitive to changes in the price of the underlying and frequent delta-hedging will be required.

While the underlying does have a delta of one, it has *no* gamma. All long options have positive gamma, and all short options have negative gamma. Gamma is greatest in near-the-money options. It diminishes the further in or out of the money you go. Gamma varies with the time remaining until expiration. For an at-the-money option, gamma increases as expiration approaches. For options that are deep in or out of the money, gamma will fall dramatically as expiration approaches.

Gamma is important as it helps us understand how our portfolio will behave for larger movements—delta is not as informative for large market moves. Delta-neutrality provides protection against small movements in the price of the underlying, while gamma-neutrality provides protection between larger movements between rebalancing.

Other Second Order Greeks

Vanna: A second-order derivative of the option value, once to the underlying spot price and once to volatility. It is mathematically equivalent to DdeltaDvol, the sensitivity of the option delta with respect to change in volatility. It is also known as DvegaDspot.

$$\text{Vanna}: \frac{\partial \Delta}{\partial \sigma} \sim \frac{\partial \nu}{\partial S} \sim \frac{\partial^2 V}{\partial S \partial \sigma}$$

Vomma: A second-order derivative of the option value with respect to the volatility, or the rate of change of vega as volatility changes (also known as volga).

$$\text{Vomma} = \frac{\partial \nu}{\partial \sigma} = \frac{\partial^2 V}{\partial \sigma^2}$$

Charm: A second-order derivative of the option value, once to price and once to the passage of time. It is mathematically equivalent to the derivative of theta with respect to the underlying's price. It is sometimes referred to as DdeltaDtime.

$$\text{Charm} = -\frac{\partial \Delta}{\partial \tau} = \frac{\partial \Theta}{\partial S} = -\frac{\partial^2 V}{\partial S \partial \tau}$$

Veta: A second-order derivative of the option value, once to volatility and once to time. Veta measures the rate of change in the vega with respect to the passage of time. It is sometimes referred to as DvegaDtime.

$$\text{Veta} = \frac{\partial \nu}{\partial \tau} = \frac{\partial^2 V}{\partial \sigma \, \partial \tau}$$

Further Greeks, third- and fourth-order, can be calculated but are beyond the needs of this book. Many options traders will use additional Greeks, but once you understand how the Greeks are calculated and work, you can see how to calculate a third-order Greek like Speed (the rate of change in Gamma with respect to changes in the underlying price).

Greeks and Moneyness

Several of the Greeks, as well as the time value of options, are highest when ATM, as Figure 8.6 shows.

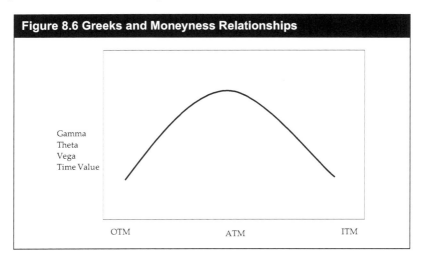

Figure 8.6 Greeks and Moneyness Relationships

145

Neutral Portfolios

As we have seen, by using a stock and an option, a trader can create a delta-neutral portfolio. If a trader wishes to further reduce sensitivities to other factors such as gamma, they could do this by adding another option to the portfolio. A portfolio of a stock and a single option could never be gamma neutral. Once a trader adds an additional option and constructs a delta gamma neutral portfolio, they would still be affected by other factors such as interest rates and volatility. In general, for each Greek they wish to hedge, they would need to add at least one additional option to the portfolio.

In the real world, it is very difficult, if not impossible, to hedge out all of your Greeks. It may be very difficult to find the correct option to hedge the portfolio, and even if it could be found, liquidity and transaction costs could be so high that putting together such a portfolio would make no economic sense. In practice, professional options traders flatten out their deltas if they wish, and hedge it once or twice a day, after that they monitor their other Greeks and take corrective action as necessary.

Portfolios of Options and the Underlying

The Greeks are additive in a linear manner. This means that the total delta exposure for all the options on a given underlying can be found by adding the delta of each individual option.

For example, if you are short 200 shares, long 5 calls with a delta of 0.5 and short 2 puts with a -0.2 delta you have a net delta equivalent to 90 shares.

$$-200 + (5 \times 100 \times 0.5) - (2 \times 100 \times -0.2) = 90$$

(In this example, each option is assumed to control 100 shares)

This approach works for delta, gamma, and theta. The net position rho may also be obtained by summing the rho of each option only if all options have the same maturity. Net position Greeks for vega, vanna and volga can be complicated as each different strike and expiration will have a different volatility (see the section on volatility surface in Chapter 11). For options with the same expirations and similar strikes these Greeks can be summed.

Chapter 8 Questions

1. Why might options traders be interested in calculating their Greeks?

2. What is the difference between a first-order and second-order Greek?

3. If a call option has a delta of 0.7, what is the delta of a put option on the same underlying with the same strike price and same expiration?

4. As the price of an underlying rises, what should happen to the delta of a call option on that underlying? What should happen to the delta of a put option on the same stock? Explain.

5. If you owned a call option on XYZ stock with a delta of 0.5, how much would you expect the call price to change if XYZ went up 0.5% in a day? How much would you expect the call price to change if the stock price moved up 25% in a day? Explain.

6. If you were long 100 shares of XYZ stock, long an XYZ call option with a delta of 0.6 and short an XYZ put option with a delta of -0.5 what is your portfolio delta (all options control 100 shares)?

7. In terms of option Greeks, what is theta?

8. If you are long two call options on XYZ stock, one expires in one month and the other expires in 6 months, which will have the most theta? Will you be losing money or gaining money each day due to theta? Explain.

9. What is the definition of gamma?

10. How does the concept of options vega fit in with the assumptions of the Black-Scholes option pricing formula?

11. How might a trader hedge their exposure to theta?

12. Is the rho of an options book always additive?

13. Suppose you are a trader and you would like to flatten the delta of your portfolio. You hold the following positions currently on a particular underlying: short 300 shares, long 9 calls with a delta of 0.4 and short 4 puts with a −0.15 delta. You are able to trade additional options on the same underlying or to trade in the underlying to get into a delta neutral position. Outline two ways you can do this.

14. How might a person using binomial trees to price an option calculate the gamma on an option that they price?

Chapter 9

DYNAMIC HEDGING OF OPTIONS

Dynamic hedging is an approach used by options traders to hedge their options positions. Because this approach involves adjusting the hedge as the underlying asset moves it is referred to as dynamic hedging. While dynamic hedging is important to understand as a hedging technique, it is more important to understand it because of the link between this hedging technique and options pricing theory. Once you understand how dynamic hedging works, you can understand how the various options pricing techniques work and understand why options traders think about options as volatility bets rather than bets on the future price of an underlying security.

A *replicating portfolio* for a given asset or series of cash flows is a portfolio of assets designed to replicate the cash flows or market values of another asset in all market scenarios. The idea is that if you can find a replicating portfolio for a given asset, this portfolio must then be priced the same as the asset it replicates, otherwise an arbitrage opportunity would exist. If there is a replicating portfolio for an option made up of the underlying stock and a bond for example, we can then use the prices of those instruments to work out the fair value of our option. If the replicating portfolio requires constant adjustment (dynamic hedging) then the price of the option should relate to the cost of creating this dynamic portfolio.

Replicating portfolios can occur in two ways: *static replication*, where the portfolio has the same cash flows as the asset in question and no changes to the portfolio need to be made to maintain this; and *dynamic replication*, where the stand alone portfolio does not necessarily have the same cash flows as the asset It seeks to replicate, but once the trading strategy underlying the replication is followed the cashflows of the portfolio match the cashflows of the underlying asset perfectly. Dynamic replication requires continual adjustment, as the asset and portfolio are only assumed to behave similarly for small market movements. The notion of a replicating portfolio is fundamental to options pricing, which assumes that market prices are arbitrage-free as arbitrage opportunities are exploited by constructing replicating portfolios and trading one against the other to profit from price discrepancies.

One of the most important things to understand about call and put options and their pricing is that their payoffs can be replicated by following a trading strategy in the underlying—without entering into an options position at all. This trading strategy, which we touched on earlier is known as dynamic replication. The fact that this can be done validates our methods of option pricing, and allows a trader or arbitrageur to generate an offsetting (hedging) set of cash flows precisely linked to an option's cash flows by actively trading the underlying, and to trade the option if they feel the market is not pricing it correctly.

As mentioned early on, options existed long before mathematical methods for pricing them did. Once the models came along, options traded at roughly the same prices as they had before. The big difference was that the volume of traded options exploded. This is not because the options pricing models made options more accessible to the public, but because the options pricing models were grounded in the idea that you could price an option in terms of the price of the underlying and you could hedge the risk of having bought or sold an option by trading the underlying against the option.

Options prices did not really change very much after the

introduction of the pricing formulas because pricing is driven by market supply and demand dynamics. All of our pricing methods include an assumed figure in the formula, which is σ or volatility. In reality, market forces push implied volatility up and down second by second.

Once traders had a formula that showed them how to dynamically replicate the payoff of an option, they were much more willing to buy and sell them as they could hedge out most of the risk.

The Dynamic Replication of a Call Option

From our last chapter, delta Δ is the amount the options price changes for a one unit change in the price of the underlying. A portfolio is delta neutral if

$$\Delta_{portfolio} = \sum N_i \Delta_i = 0$$

meaning that the delta of a portfolio is equivalent to the weighted sum of the deltas of the portfolio constituents Is equal to zero.

Delta-neutral portfolios are of interest because they are a way to hedge out the risk of an option or portfolio of options. If, for example, you sell one European call option, which by convention is always applied to 100 shares of stock, whose delta is 0.6, how can you get your trade to be delta neutral?

$$n_c \Delta_{call} + n_s \Delta_S = -1(0.61) + n_s(1) = 0$$

We need to hold 0.6 × 100 shares of stock, or 60 shares, to be delta neutral.

If you were to dynamically hedge the above call option, you would sell the call, and buy Δ times the number of shares covered by the option. Each time the price of the underlying stock changes, the delta of the option of the stock will change. As the delta of the stock changes, you will find yourself buying and selling stock. If the realized volatility of the stock over the period covered by the option is equal to the implied volatility of the call option you sold, you will find that your losses from this constant buying and selling of the underlying stock will exactly offset the premium that you took in when you sold the call option.

When we look at the payoff diagrams of a call option we can see that it looks a little bit like the payoff of being long a stock with a stop loss (stop order) in place. If the stock price goes up, we get a return somewhat like that of the underlying stock, and if the price falls a lot, it looks like we get stopped out[6]. With an option, if the price rises again, we find ourselves with the payoff of being long the stock again. For the replicating portfolio to work it must trade in such a manner.

If you look at how delta changes as the stock price moves up and down, you will see that, roughly speaking, an at the money call has a delta of around 0.5. The dotted line is the tangent line to the options valuation, and it is also the delta for a given share price on the x-axis, so owning the option is a bit like owning half a share times the number of shares covered by the option. As the underlying goes up in price the delta increases, and it becomes like owning more and more of the stock as it gets deeper and deeper into the money (see Figure 9.1). As the price of the stock falls, the delta also falls and you find yourself owning less and less of the stock in your dynamic hedging as the option moves out of the money. Unlike being long a stock with a stop loss, as the price falls you do not dump all of your stock in one go, you sell it in small increments over time as the price is moving down, to maintain your appropriate delta hedge ratio. Equally, as the stock price rises, you find yourself buying more and more stock in small increments to maintain your appropriate hedge.

---

[6] Stopped out is a term used by traders referring to a stop order being executed by the broker, exiting their initial stock position. Refer to 'Types of orders' in Chapter 2.

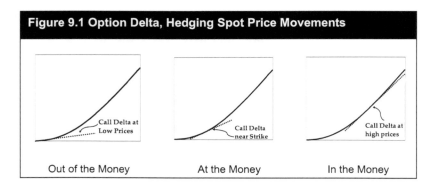

Figure 9.1 Option Delta, Hedging Spot Price Movements

Call Delta at Low Prices — Out of the Money

Call Delta near Strike — At the Money

Call Delta at high prices — In the Money

Gamma and Dynamic Hedging

The above example helps to give you some insight into gamma, in particular for an at-the-money option very close to expiration. Suppose you wish to replicate an at-the-money call option on expiration day and the option has a strike price of $50, the underlying is at $50. In order to replicate the payoff of the option, you buy 100 shares of stock every time the price of the underlying ticks above $50 and sell 100 shares every time it ticks below $50. As you can see in this example, gamma is at its highest for at-the-money options on expiration as delta quickly ticks between 1 and 0 with up and down moves in the underlying. Because of this, high gamma on expiration day for at-the-money options, a huge amount of the trading in the underlying stock can be options traders delta hedging their options, with no real long term view as to the long term prospects of the stock. For this reason, on expiration day you will often see stocks becoming pinned to high open-interest options strikes.

What is Volatility Arbitrage?

As you can see above, if a trader was to put on a delta-neutral options position and dynamically hedge it, their risk no longer relates to the price direction of the underlying stock.

The trader instead would have exposure to the risks described by the other Greeks covered in the last chapter. The main reason a trader would want to have a delta-neutral portfolio is because of the trader's view on volatility. The trader either thinks that the implied volatility built into the options price is too high or too low. The trader is only going to sell options when they think that they are getting paid too much for them, and buy options when they think that they are priced too cheaply in the market at a given time.

Let's look at how a volatility trader can make money from a delta-neutral portfolio if their forecast of volatility is more accurate than that of the market's forecast of volatility, the implied volatility of traded options in the market.

We will start with a situation where a directional trader buys 1000 put options. suppose each option covers one share, from a volatility trader on a stock that is trading at $20. The directional trader is buying these puts because they expect the stock price to fall a lot. The volatility trader is selling these puts, but is indifferent as to which direction the underlying moves, as they can hedge that; rather, the volatility trader just feels that the implied volatility being used to price the option is too high and thus that the option price is too high (see Figure 9.2).

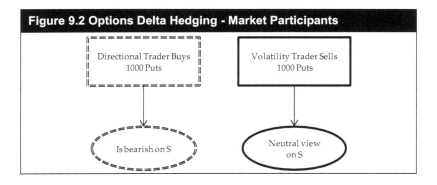

In this example we will imagine that the delta of these puts is −0.3. For this reason, the volatility trader will sell 300 shares right as they enter into this strategy.

$$-0.3 \times 1000 = -300$$

No sooner than our two traders have taken their initial positions, imagine that the stock price falls 1%. This is clearly good for the directional trader, as money is made on the puts as the price of the underlying falls. The volatility trader who had sold the puts will be taking a loss on the puts equal to the gain that the directional trader is making, but they are also short 300 shares in the underlying and will have gained $300 \times \$0.20 = \$60$, and being delta neutral, we can assume that the puts fell in value by about $60. So at this point in the game, the volatility trader has broken even and the directional trader is up $60 (see Figure 9.3).

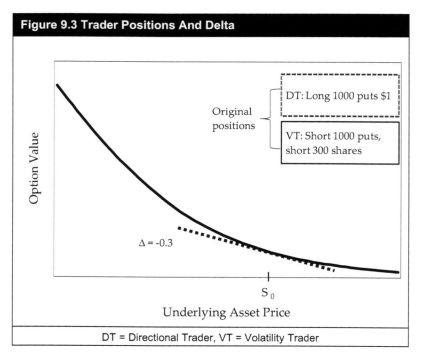

Figure 9.3 Trader Positions And Delta

Original positions

DT: Long 1000 puts $1

VT: Short 1000 puts, short 300 shares

$\Delta = -0.3$

S_0

Underlying Asset Price

Option Value

DT = Directional Trader, VT = Volatility Trader

The delta of the option will, however, have changed because of this 1% fall in the stock price, so our volatility trader will have to recalculate the delta and rehedge exposure. Positions after the underlying price falls by 1% are illustrated in Figure 9.4.

When the volatility trader recalculates delta, it is now −0.4, so in order to remain delta neutral, they must sell an additional 100 shares, now short 400 shares.

Once the volatility trader has rehedged, the market then rises 2%. This will cause a loss for the directional trader who is long puts and only makes money when the price of the underlying falls. The volatility trader will make money on the short puts, but will lose money on the 400 shares held short as a delta hedge. Positions after underlying price rises by 2% are illustrated in Figure 9.5.

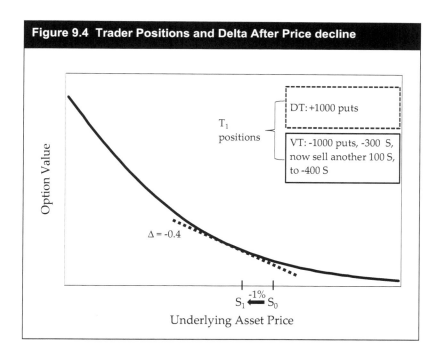

Figure 9.4 Trader Positions and Delta After Price decline

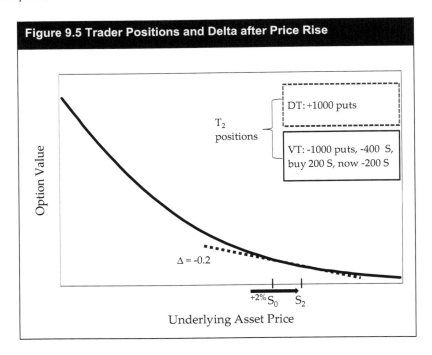

Figure 9.5 Trader Positions and Delta after Price Rise

Once again, our volatility trader will calculate delta, and this time it is −0.2. The volatility trader is short 400 shares, and should only be short 200, so must buy back 200 shares in the market in order to return to being delta neutral.

In the above example, the volatility trader's profits and losses remain muted relative to those of the directional trader as long as they stay well delta hedged. The directional trader's profits and losses are quite clearly driven by the direction of the underlying stock.

In the example, the volatility trader sells stock as the market falls and buys stock back when the market rises. The more this happens, the more the volatility trader's hedge will lose money. On the other hand, they received premium at inception of the trade from the directional trader from selling them the puts. If the stock moves around exactly as much as would be expected by the implied volatility, the volatility trader should lose an amount of money on the hedge that exactly equals the premium paid by the directional trader. When realized volatility equals implied volatility, the dynamic trading strategy has a P&L that is exactly offsetting the initial price of the option.

The volatility trader makes money if they buy options or buy volatility where realized volatility ends up being higher than the implied volatility of the option they trade initially. They can also make money when they sell options or sell volatility where realized volatility ends up being lower than implied volatility of the option they trade initially.

Volatility traders are hoping to crystallize the difference between their view of projected volatility on an underlying and that priced into an option in terms of implied volatility. In practice, however, volatility traders do not hedge and rehedge their positions continuously, as the Black-Scholes model suggests one can or should. Realistically, rehedging occurs either at set time intervals, hourly, often just daily, or when the trader has pre-established thresholds of price movements. Perhaps they will determine for themselves set percentage increases or decreases in the underlying's price that will trigger the trader to adjust a hedge. You can imagine that in practice this can give rise to large differences in profitability between two similarly nondirectionally motivated volatility traders.

Chapter 9 Questions

1. Explain the trading strategy that would allow a trader to replicate the payoff of a call option by only trading in the underlying stock.

2. How did the appearance of options pricing formulas affect the popularity of options and why?

3. If an investor was long an XYZ call option with a delta of 0.4, how might they flatten out their delta? Why might they wish to do this?

4. How is does gamma change for options as expiration gets closer? Is it affected by the moneyness of the option?

5. Are options a zero sum game in a world where dynamic replication exists?

6. Suppose an options contract is entered into between two counterparties, one is a directional trader, the other is a volatility trader (taking no view on the direction of the underlying, but planning to delta-hedge the option to maturity). The directional trader has purchased an ATM call option, with a delta of 0.52 for $3, with a strike of $50. Suppose the underlying rises the next day by 1%. Approximately how much money will each of the traders have made (or lost) from this move?

7. In reference to the prior question, what was the volatility trader's view of the implied volatility of the call option at the time they entered into the transaction?

8. Again referencing Question 6's volatility transaction, each time the underlying rises, what actions will the volatility trader have to take to flatten the portfolio? Alternatively, each time the underlying falls, what actions will the volatility trader have to take to flatten the portfolio? Overall does the volatility trader expect to make or lose money on their delta-hedging trades

(judged separately from the profits or losses on the options trade)?

9. Again, referencing Question 6's volatility transaction: Suppose the day after the options trade the underlying stock rallies by 20% and then remains there until the option expires. Approximately how much does each trader make or lose?

Chapter 10

OPTIONS ON VARIOUS UNDERLYINGS

Options on Stock Indices

A stock market index is a method of measuring the price movements of a basket of stocks in a market. Many indices are cited by the media and are used as benchmarks to measure the performance of portfolios such as mutual funds. Some are price indices and some are total return indices, meaning that they include reinvested dividends over time.

There are a number of different index types. National indices represent the performance of the stock market of a given nation. Sector indices track the performance of specific industry sectors in the market. Ethical indices include only those companies that satisfy certain ecological, religious, or social criteria.

Index options exist on broad-based indices like the S&P500 or the Russell 3000. They also exist on more narrowly based indices like mining indices or semiconductor indices. The global market for exchange-traded stock market index options is notionally valued by the Bank for International Settlements at hundreds of billions per year. When OTC options are added to that, you can see that it is a very large market indeed.

An index option is a financial derivative that gives the holder the right, but not the obligation, to buy or sell a basket of stocks, such as the S&P500, at a pre-agreed price on a specified date. An index option is similar to other options contracts, the difference being the underlying instruments are indexes. Index options are typically cash settled.

The Uses of Index Options

There are two main reasons that investors will pursue index options.

1. Portfolio insurance: Investors with large stock portfolios may wish to insure their downside risk by buying put options.
2. Speculation: Portfolio managers may wish to use index options to speculate on the direction of the overall market, or on the volatility of the overall market.

Beta in Hedging

Beta (β) is a measure of the volatility or systemic risk of an investment arising from exposure to general market movements as opposed to idiosyncratic factors. Beta specifically gives the volatility ratio multiplied by the correlation of the plotted data over a given historical timeframe. The market portfolio of all investable assets has a beta of exactly 1. A beta above 1 generally means that the asset is both volatile and that it tends to move up and down with the market. Negative betas are possible for investments that tend to go down when the market goes up, and vice versa.

To calculate beta, you need historical returns data for the asset and returns data for the index. Using the standard linear regression formula, the slope of the fitted line from the linear least-squares calculation is the estimated beta.

A portfolio with a beta of 1 and a similar dividend yield to the index can be expected to mimic the index in terms of returns. An S&P500 index option has a multiplier of 250—if the index is at 2000, each

S&P500 index option would have a notional value of 2000 × 250 = $500,000. A portfolio manager wishing to hedge a $1 million portfolio of stocks with a beta of 1 could buy 2 S&P500 put options. When the beta of the portfolio is not equal to 1, the minimum variance hedge ratio discussed in Chapter 2 can be used to calculate the number of contracts required (see Figure 10.1).

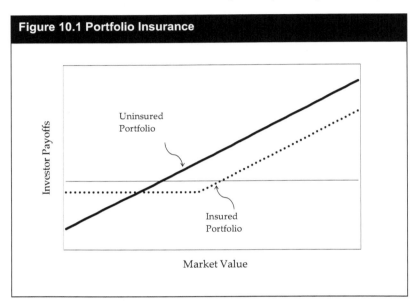

Figure 10.1 Portfolio Insurance

Index Options and Dividends

For options on indices, it is reasonable to make the simplifying assumption that dividends are paid continuously, and that the dividend amount is proportional to the level of the index. This allows us to use the Merton model to price stock index options.

We assume that the index price follows a geometric Brownian motion and the dividend payment paid over the time period ($t,t+dt$) is modeled as

$$qS_tdt$$

For some constant q (the dividend yield)

Under this formulation, the arbitrage-free price implied by the Black-Scholes model can be shown to be

$$C(S_0, t) = e^{-r(T-t)}[FN(d_1) - KN(d_2)]$$

and

$$P(S_0, t) = e^{-r(T-t)}[KN(-d_2) - FN(-d_1)]$$

where the modified forward price occurring in the terms d_1, d_2 is

$$F = S_0 e^{(r-q)(T-t)}$$

$$d_1 = \frac{1}{\sigma\sqrt{T-t}}\left[\ln\left(\frac{S_0}{K}\right) + (r - q + \frac{1}{2}\sigma^2)(T-t)\right]$$

therefore

$$d_2 = d_1 - \sigma\sqrt{T-t}$$

Options on Futures Contracts

Options on futures are very widely traded, and they require the delivery of an underlying futures contract upon exercise. When a call on a futures contract is exercised, the underlying futures contract is delivered, but a cash settlement is also made for the difference between the most recent futures settlement price and the strike price. Similarly, if a put on a futures contract is exercised, the underlying short futures contract is delivered, along with a cash settlement for the difference between the most recent futures settlement price and the strike price. Options on futures are attractive to investors when it is simpler to deliver futures contracts rather than the underlying asset itself, which is the case when the effective underlying is, for example, 500 individual stocks.

Options on futures are available on financial futures, commodity futures, and interest rate futures.

The *Black model* is used for pricing options on futures. It can also be used for pricing bond options, interest rate caps and floors, and swaptions. The Black formula is similar to the Black–Scholes formula except that the spot price of the underlying S_0 is replaced by a discounted futures price F and $q = r$

the Black formula states the price for a European call option of maturity T on a futures contract with strike price K and delivery date T' (with T' ≥ ≥T) is

$$c = e^{-rT}[FN(d_1) - KN(d_2)]$$

the put price is

$$p = e^{-rT}[KN(-d_2) - FN(-d_1)]$$

where

$$d_1 = \frac{\ln(F/K) + (\sigma^2/2)T}{\sigma\sqrt{T}}$$

$$d_2 = \frac{\ln(F/K) - (\sigma^2/2)T}{\sigma\sqrt{T}} = d_1 - \sigma\sqrt{T}$$

When a European futures contract expires at the same time as the futures contract, $F_t = S_t$, an option on a future should be equivalent to an option on the spot. If the option matures before the underlying future, it should trade at a premium to an option on spot in a market where futures prices are higher than spot prices, and at a discount to an option on spot where futures prices are lower than spot prices.[7]

Options on Foreign Exchange

A foreign exchange option is a derivative where the owner has the

---

[7] For more detail on this point see the section on Backwardation and Contango in Chapter 2.

right but not the obligation to exchange money denominated in one currency into another currency at a pre-agreed exchange rate on a specified date. European and American options on foreign exchange are actively traded on both exchanges and OTC. Companies frequently use them to hedge foreign exchange risk, and they are commonly used to speculate on the price and volatility of various foreign exchange pairs. The foreign exchange options market is mostly an OTC market.

A GBP/USD foreign exchange call option, can also be viewed as being a USD/GBP put option, as they each give the option owner the right but not the obligation to exchange a certain amount of US dollars for British pounds at a pre-agreed exchange rate on a specified date.

The Black-Scholes model can be modified to price options on foreign exchange. The modified Black-Scholes model was developed in 1983 by Garman and Kohlhagen and is known as the Garman-Kohlhagen model. It is a modification of the Black-Scholes model which accounts for the different interest rates of each currency.

You can think of options on currencies as being an options position with an annual percentage dividend embedded in the form of the foreign currencies' risk-free rate.

The domestic currency valuation of a foreign exchange call option is:

$$c = S_0 e^{-r_f T} N(d_1) - K e^{-r_d T} N(d_2)$$

The domestic currency valuation of a foreign exchange put option is:

$$p = K e^{-r_d T} N(-d_2) - S_0 e^{-r_f T} N(-d_1)$$

where

$$d_1 = \frac{\ln\left(S_0/K\right) + \left(r_d - r_f + \sigma^2/2\right)T}{\sigma\sqrt{T}}$$

and

$$d_2 = d_1 - \sigma\sqrt{T}$$

r_d is the domestic risk-free rate

r_f is foreign risk-free rate

σ is the volatility of the exchange rate

Chapter 10 Questions

1. Explain what stock indices are and why they exist. Explain why investors may wish to trade index-based derivatives.

2. What is beta, how is the concept of beta valuable to a hedger?

3. In what way are dividends in a stock index different to dividends on single stocks?

4. Explain why interest payments on a foreign currency can be treated like a dividend on a common stock?

5. How might you adjust a binomial tree on an underlying that makes discrete payments?

6. If an American and a European call option on the same underlying which are otherwise identical have exactly the same option prices, what does this reveal about the underlying? Explain.

7. A stock index is trading at 1000, with 20% volatility and the risk-free interest rate is at 5%. It will pay a dividend of 40 index units in 40 days. At-the-money calls and puts are available on the index that expire in 120 days. Find the American and European options prices of the two options using two-period binomial trees.

8. A portfolio is currently worth $100m and has a beta of 1.1. The S&P500 is currently trading at 2000. How might a put option on the index with a strike of 1900 be used to insure the portfolio?

9. An index currently is trading at 1000 and has a volatility of 20% per annum. The risk-free rate of interest is 5% per annum and the index has a dividend yield of 3% per annum. Calculate the price of a three-month European put option with an exercise price of 900. Calculate the delta of this option.

10. Would you expect the volatility of a stock index to be higher, lower, or equal to the average volatility of its component stocks? Explain your reasoning.

Chapter 11

THE VOLATILITY SMILE

The *volatility smile* is a pattern of implied volatility for a series of options that have the same underlying, the same expiration date, but different strike prices. When implied volatility is plotted against strike prices, a line is created that slopes upward on either end, hence the term "smile." Volatility smiles should not occur based on standard Black-Scholes option theory, which requires a completely flat volatility curve. The pattern displays different characteristics for different markets and results from the probability of extreme moves. Equity options traded in American markets did not show a volatility smile before the Crash of 1987 but began showing one afterward.

Several theories exist to explain the existence of volatility smiles. The simplest explanation is that demand is greater for options that are in-the-money or out-of-the-money as opposed to those at-the-money. This greater demand increases their prices versus what would otherwise be predicted in a model like Black-Scholes and this price increase manifests itself through an increase in implied volatility, the only unobservable variable in the model, compared to the ATM options. Others suggest that more advanced approaches to pricing options have led to out-of-the-money options becoming priced more expensively to account for risk of extreme market events. Another theory is that the market for options is driven largely by investors aiming to "insure" their equity holdings, particularly since the 1987 crash, and that those buyers are natural buyers of out-of-the-money put options. It is also reasonable to believe that as a company's equity value declines, its leverage increases. This means that the company is riskier and thus the implied volatility should be higher (see Figure 11.1).

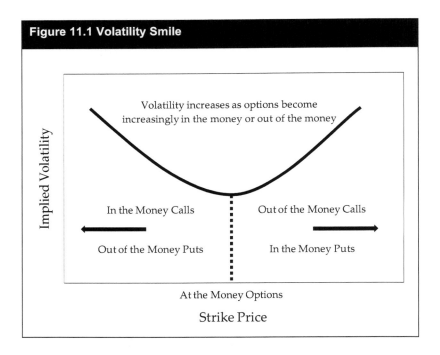

Figure 11.1 Volatility Smile

Volatility increases as options become increasingly in the money or out of the money

Implied Volatility

In the Money Calls

Out of the Money Calls

Out of the Money Puts

In the Money Puts

At the Money Options

Strike Price

When the volatility smile is plotted for equity markets it is typically downward sloping and the term "volatility skew" is often used to describe it (see Figure 11.2). The implied volatility for high-strike equity options is typically lower than for at-the-money equity options, which are in turn typically lower than for low strike options. Sometimes the term "smirk" is used to describe a skewed smile.

For other markets, such as foreign exchange options, where the typical graph turns up at either end, the more familiar term "volatility smile" is used. In-the-money and out-of-the-money volatility in currency pairs are priced in live trading options as being higher than spot volatility—causing a smile.

If an underlying is observed to typically have higher volatility when its price rises, then its volatility Smile/Skew will be different than that of most equities. It will be said to have a negative skew.

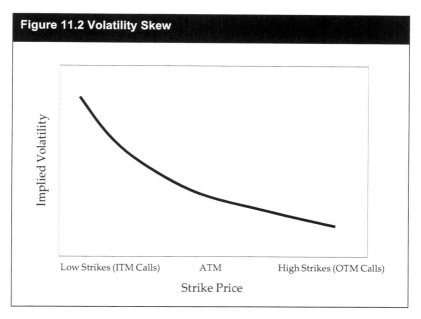

Figure 11.2 Volatility Skew

What are Implied Distributions?

Volatility smiles help to take into account that the behavior of stock prices in the real world may be different from the geometric Brownian motion and lognormal distributions assumed in many option pricing methodologies. The smile in options implies a distribution different to the standard normal distribution used in the Black-Scholes model, and as such adjusts for one of the most commonly pointed out flaws in the model.

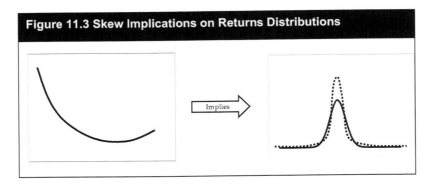

Figure 11.3 Skew Implications on Returns Distributions

The volatility skew directly implies a distribution of prices that the market believes a given underlying will follow over the life of a given series of options. This can be plotted as such (see Figure 11.3). For any terminal probability distribution *p(S)* at expiration *T*, we have the model-free formula for the call price *C(K)* as a function of strike *K*:

$$C = e^{-rT} \int_0^\infty (S - K)^+ p(S) dS$$

Therefore

$$e^{rT} \frac{\partial C}{\partial K} = \int_K^\infty (-1) \cdot p(S) dS$$

And by the fundamental theorem of calculus:

$$e^{rT} \frac{\partial^2 C}{\partial K^2} = p(K)$$

Consequently, all you need, in order to find the value of *p(x)* for any *x*, is the second derivative of call prices at strike *x*. You can use a fitted skew, such as a polynomial fit, to the available volatility values at the given maturity. Once you have a continuous skew *σ(K)* then you need to find

$$\frac{\partial^2}{\partial x^2}\bigg| BS_{\text{Call}}(S_0, x, \sigma(x), r, T, q)$$

evaluated at *x=K* which can be done by finite differencing, allowing you to plot the implied distribution (see Figure 11.4).

The *kurtosis* or *tailedness* of a distribution is not the only thing that the options market will be adjusting for. Kurtosis in statistics is a calculation of the nature of the tails of a distribution curve. Leptokurtic distributions are considered to have positive excess kurtosis, or fatter tails (more examples of and greater outlier positions than would be expected from a normal distribution). Platykurtic distributions have negative excess kurtosis, or thinner tails, which means that tail data points are fewer and or less extreme than the tails of the normal distribution curve. For certain types of underlying, a normal distribution may be entirely inappropriate. In periods when a market jump is expected but the direction of the jump is unknown, such as during political elections, or for a pharmaceutical company who is hoping to get FDA approval for an important drug compound, a stock-index option which matures after the event should reflect a bimodal underlying distribution (see Figure 11.5).

Figure 11.4 Implied vs. Lognormal Distributions

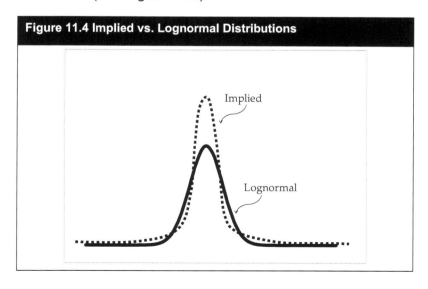

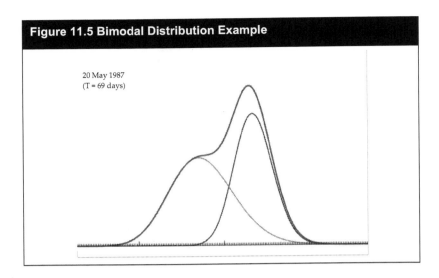

Figure 11.5 Bimodal Distribution Example

20 May 1987
(T = 69 days)

Figure 11.5 The implied distribution of the FTSE100 in advance of the 1987 British Elections indicating a nearly bimodal distribution (Gemmill and Saflekos, Bank for International Settlements).

When a cash merger is announced, one would not expect the returns of the stock price to be lognormally distributed, as either the cash merger will go through and the stock holder will receive a fixed amount of money, or the merger will fail and the stock price will lose its deal premium. In addition, other suitors may arrive and make an offer above the terms of the initial deal. In the case of announced mergers, option prices imply a distribution which is hump shaped and volatility that is increasing in event time.

Trading Terminology

Market practitioners usually use the term "implied volatility" to describe at-the-money option volatility. Adjustments to this value are undertaken by incorporating the values of *risk reversals* (an investment strategy that amounts to both buying and selling out-of-money options simultaneously) and *butterflies* (a combination of a bull spread and a bear spread) to better describe the various volatility measures that are being used for options with a delta different from0.5 (see Chapter 4).

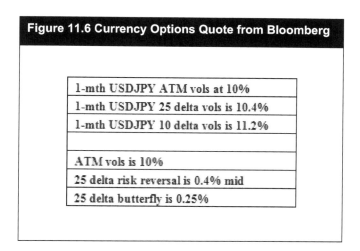

Figure 11.6 Currency Options Quote from Bloomberg

1-mth USDJPY ATM vols at 10%
1-mth USDJPY 25 delta vols is 10.4%
1-mth USDJPY 10 delta vols is 11.2%
ATM vols is 10%
25 delta risk reversal is 0.4% mid
25 delta butterfly is 0.25%

Figure 11.6 is an example of a currency options quote highlighting some of the terminology explained above. Note that "prices" are all referring to the implied volatility levels, as opposed to option premiums.

What Does Options Skew Tell us?

Options skew, which is constantly changing throughout the day as options trade, can be viewed as a measure of fear in the marketplace at a given time. For example, suppose the S&P500 index skew steepens significantly over a trading day. This means that the downside strikes' implied volatility is increasing versus the at-the-money strikes or upside price strikes. This may imply that market participants are growing increasingly concerned about a sudden drop in equity prices and thus they are willing to pay a lot more to protect themselves against downside risks in the markets.

What is the Term Structure of Volatility?

In addition to the volatility smile, options of different maturities also display characteristic differences in implied volatility. This is referred to as the *term structure of volatility*. A few things affect the term structure of volatility. The main effect relates to the implied impact of upcoming market events. For example, an option maturing after a company's earnings announcement would be expected to have higher implied volatility than one expiring right before such an event. Options on US Treasury bill futures show an increase in implied volatility just before meetings of the Federal Reserve Board when changes in short-term interest rates may be announced.

If short-dated options have unusually high implied volatility, the term structure on that underlying will likely be a declining curve. This means there is lower implied volatility for longer-dated options. Conversely, if the implied volatility is unusually high for options on an underlying, the term structure will likely be rising, meaning there is higher implied volatility for longer-dated options. There isn't necessarily a "standard" term structure of volatility curve. Short-dated implied volatility tends to exhibit a greater range than long-dated volatility.

Much like with the volatility smile, the market incorporates many types of expected events into the term structure of volatility. For example, the impact of the results of a drug trial can be seen in both the implied volatility smile and the term structure of implied volatility for pharmaceutical stocks.

The shape of the volatility smile can depend on the option maturity. Frequently the smile will become less pronounced as the option maturity increases.

What is the Volatility Surface?

The *volatility surface* is a plot of implied volatility as a function of both strike price and time to maturity.

The implied volatility surface shows the implied volatility smile and the term structure of implied volatility simultaneously. The implied volatilities for recently traded options are plotted, and linear interpolation is used to show all other data points (see Figures 11.7 and 11.8). When a new option has to be valued, perhaps for a strike that has not yet traded, or a maturity that is not yet available, traders can find an appropriate volatility by finding its position on the volatility surface.

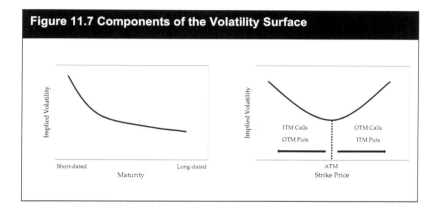

Figure 11.7 Components of the Volatility Surface

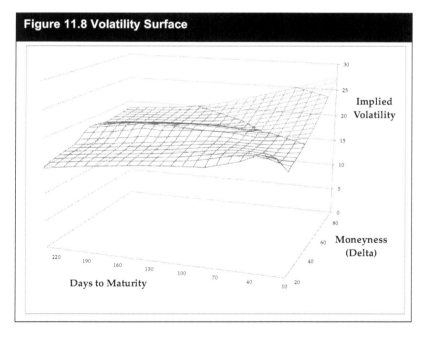

Figure 11.8 Volatility Surface

How do Traders Model Volatility?

One of the assumptions of the Black-Scholes model is that volatility is constant over the life of the derivative, and unaffected by the changes in the price level of the underlying security. *Local volatility models* and *stochastic volatility models* are approaches that aim to resolve these shortcomings.

A local volatility model is one that treats volatility as a function of both the current asset level and of time. As such, a local volatility model is a generalization of the Black-Scholes model, where the volatility is a constant. Derman and Kani described and implemented a local volatility function to model instantaneous volatility and then used this function at each node in a binomial options pricing model. This approach successfully produced option valuations consistent with all market prices across strikes and expirations. The continuous-time equations used in local volatility models were later developed by Bruno Dupire.

Stochastic volatility models treat the underlying security's volatility as a random process, governed by state variables such as the price level of the underlying security, the tendency of volatility to mean revert, and the variance of the volatility process itself, among others. Once a particular stochastic volatility model is chosen, it is then calibrated against existing market data.

Modeling the volatility surface is an active area of research in quantitative finance, and some pricing models as mentioned above partially address this issue. A number of difficulties exist in empirical research on how well various options pricing models work. Any statistical hypothesis on how options are priced is a joint hypothesis on how well the options model works and how efficient markets are. There are considerable difficulties in working with historical options price data, as often options are widely traded when at-the-money, and then become quite illiquid once they are away from the money. Often option price data will not be synchronous with the closing price data used by a researcher. Many options, even on highly liquid underlyings, are illiquid to the extent that they can have a number of trading days with no transactions. On days when transactions do occur, they may not have occurred at the market close. The option's closing price will show as its "last" transaction price for the day, which could have potentially occurred hours away from the settle price of the underlying. The relationship between the option and the underlying's settle prices are therefore often incongruous data points. Stale prices are a considerable problem when analyzing live options price data.

Chapter 11 Questions

1. Are volatility smiles allowed for in the assumptions underlying the Black-Scholes model?

2. Is the volatility smile different for put and call options?

3. What is the difference between volatility smile and volatility skew?

4. Does a market with a volatility smile imply anything about the distribution of returns of the underlying?

5. What does kurtosis mean in probability theory and statistics?

6. Far out of the money options can be viewed as options on volatility. Discuss.

7. What might you expect a volatility smile to look like for a stock with a bimodal distribution?

8. A pharmaceutical company's stock is trading at $40. The results of a highly anticipated drug trial are expected to be announced in the morning, and the stock could either double or halve when the news is released. Should we expect the Black-Scholes model to give us a reasonable price on an option with two weeks left to expiration? Explain your answer.

9. Explain what information the prices of risk reversals and butterflies would give to an option trader who inquired as to the level of implied volatility in a stock?

10. If at-the-money implied volatility in the S&P500 has remained at 20 for the last month, but options skew has been slowly rising, what might that tell us about stock market expectations?

11. Why might short-dated and long-dated options trade with different levels of implied volatility?

12. Does put-call parity hold if options with different strikes and different expirations are trading at different implied volatilities?

13. Explain what a stochastic volatility model is.

Chapter 12

VOLATILITY & VARIANCE SWAPS

If you want a long position in future realized volatility, delta hedging a single option is not optimal; as soon as the stock price changes, your sensitivity to further changes in volatility is altered because of gamma. In theory, the returns associated with delta-hedging an option are fixed and are entirely based on the difference between the implied volatility of the option when it was purchased and the realized volatility of the underlying over the life of the option. In the real world, with discrete, rather than continuous delta hedging, this is not the case. Traders might choose to readjust their hedges hourly, daily, or only following pre-set percentage price movements, or otherwise. Variance and volatility swaps were created to allow investors to hedge volatility risk or speculate on implied volatility in a clean manner without the need for continuous delta hedging, which can be expensive and inefficient. The naming of these products as swaps is somewhat misleading, as they are more like forwards. This is because their payoff occurs at maturity, whereas swaps have intermediate payments.

What are Volatility Swaps?

A *volatility swap* is an over-the-counter financial derivative which allows investors to trade based on their expectations of what future realized volatility will be versus what is observed in current implied volatility. It acts like a forward contract on the future realized volatility of a given underlying asset. Volatility swaps allow investors to trade the volatility of an asset directly, much as they would trade a stock or an index. At inception of the trade, the strike is usually chosen such that the fair value of the swap is zero.

The payoff of a volatility swap is as follows:

$$N_{vol}(\sigma_{realized} - \sigma_{strike})$$

where:

N_{vol} = volatility notional
$\sigma_{realized}$ = annualized realized volatility

σ_{strike} = volatility strike

Volatility notional = vega = notional amount paid (or received) per volatility point (per 1% shift in realized standard deviation of daily returns of the underlying).

The payout of a volatility swap is the notional, multiplied by the difference between the realized volatility and the volatility strike agreed at inception. The profit and loss on a volatility swap relates only to the realized volatility of the underlying and is unaffected by any directional moves, thus it gives you a simpler and more pure volatility exposure than that achieved by manually delta hedging an option.

How are Volatility Swaps Hedged?

There is no simple replication strategy for a volatility swap. Variance rather than volatility exposure is what you get from hedged options trading. From a derivatives point of view, variance can be viewed as the primary underlying, and volatility swaps are best regarded as derivative securities on variance. Volatility, being the square root of variance, is a nonlinear function and is therefore more difficult, both theoretically and practically, to value and hedge.

The main difficulty with pricing and hedging volatility swaps is that they require a volatility of volatility (vol of vol) model, and if this model is not representative of the real world trajectory of volatility, the model's pricing will be wrong. Volatility swaps are very difficult to hedge, and so market participants moved toward trading variance swaps, as variance swaps can be statically replicated.

Volatility swaps cannot be hedged by a static portfolio of options, but they can be hedged with variance swaps. For small moves, the payouts of volatility and variance swaps can be similar (see Figure 12.1).

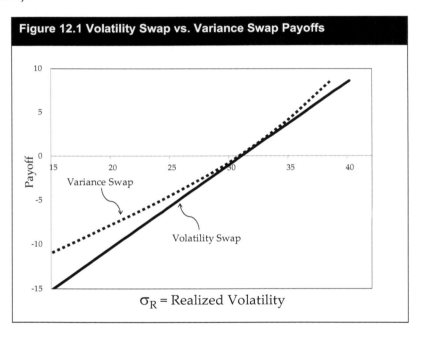

Figure 12.1 Volatility Swap vs. Variance Swap Payoffs

σ_R = Realized Volatility

The vega of a variance swap is equal to variance notional × 2σ. So a volatility swap of vega 'V' can be hedged with $V/2\sigma$ variance notional of a variance swap. As Figure 12.1 illustrates, the payoff profiles between these two instruments are slightly different. In the same way that the appropriate option hedge ratio depends on the assumed future volatility of the stock, the dynamic replication of a volatility swap requires a model for the volatility of volatility.

What are Variance Swaps?

A *variance swap* is an over-the-counter financial derivative instrument that allows investors to trade future realized variance against current implied variance. It acts like a forward contract on the future realized variance of a given underlying asset. The reason variance is used rather than volatility is that variance (volatility squared) can be replicated with a static hedge[8].

At the inception of the trade, the strike is usually chosen such that the fair value of the swap is zero. Variance swaps allow investors to speculate on or hedge risks associated with volatility. One leg of the swap will pay an amount based upon the realized variance of the price changes of the underlying product. Usually, these price changes will be daily log returns, based upon daily closing prices. The other leg of the swap will pay a fixed amount, which is the strike—quoted at the deal's inception. Thus, the net payoff to the counterparties will be the difference between these two and will be settled in cash at the expiration of the deal.

The long party receives realized variance and pays the strike variance at maturity and the short party receives the strike variance and pays realized variance at maturity.

The annualized realized variance is calculated based on a pre-specified set of sampling points over the life of the swap. Normally, an investment bank is the calculation agent for any variance swaps traded. The calculation agent usually has some discretion over how to calculate when a market disruption event occurs or the treatment of situations such as if a stock is delisted. This can lead to issues if an investor is long and short identical products facing two separate

---

[8] As opposed to requiring dynamic hedging.

investment banks. These problems are less of an issue if the counterparties are joint calculation agents.

The profit and loss on a variance swap relates only to the realized variance (volatility squared) of the underlying and is unaffected by any directional moves, thus, much like a volatility swap, it gives you a simpler and more pure volatility exposure than delta hedging an option does.

The payoff of a variance swap is convex in volatility. This means that an investor who is long a variance swap will benefit from boosted gains and discounted losses. This bias is reflected in slightly higher strike prices for variance swaps compared to volatility swaps, a phenomenon that is amplified when volatility skew is steep. The fair value of a variance swap is determined by the cost of the replicating portfolio of options. This cost, especially for index options, is significantly affected by the volatility smile or skew.

The return calculation for a variance swap on an index does not adjust for any dividend payments that are paid. This means that the dividend modeling method can affect pricing. Long dated dividends are usually modeled as a flat yield, and near-dated, and, hence, either known or relatively certain dividends are modeled discretely.

The payoff of a variance swap is as follows: $N_{var}(\sigma^2 realized - \sigma^2 strike)$

where:

N_{var} = variance notional
$\sigma^2_{realized}$ = annualized realized variance

σ^2_{strike} = variance strike

Daily returns are computed on a logarithmic basis:

$$\ln\left\{\frac{P_t}{P_{t-1}}\right\}$$

Market Conventions

For variance swaps, instead of using the standard calculation for variance, the contract terms usually set the expected return of the underlying to zero. The reason for this is that its impact on the price is minimal (the expected average daily return is $1/252^{nd}$ of an overnight borrow rate), while its omission has the benefit of making the payoff additive (3 month variance + 9 month variance in 3 months = 1 year variance).

It is a market practice to define the variance notional in volatility terms since most traders are cognizant of implied volatility levels on the underlyings they are interested in:

$$\text{Variance notional} = \frac{Vega\ Notional}{2 \cdot Strike}$$

With this adjustment, if the realized volatility is one volatility point above the strike at maturity, the payoff is approximately equal to the vega notional.

How are Variance Swaps Hedged?

In order to price variance swaps, we should first look at a replicating portfolio that captures realized variance. The cost of that portfolio should be the fair value of future realized variance. To achieve such a portfolio, you need to combine options of many strikes. A portfolio of options of all strikes, weighted in inverse proportion to the square of the strike level $\frac{1}{K^2}$ where K is the strike of the option. Each option weighted by 1 divided by its own strike squared gives an exposure to variance that is independent of stock price. Intuitively, as the stock price moves up to higher levels, each additional option of higher strike in the portfolio provides an additional contribution to variance proportional to that strike.

It takes an infinite number of strikes, appropriately weighted, to replicate a variance swap. In practice, this is neither possible nor practical. There are only a finite number of options available at any maturity and if the stock price moves outside the range of available strikes, the reduced vega of the imperfectly replicated contract will make it less responsive than a true variance swap. As long as the stock price remains within a reasonable range around the strike, trading the imperfectly replicated contract will allow variance to accrue at the correct rate.

How are Variance Swaps Priced?

Variance swaps can theoretically be hedged as described above and thus priced as a portfolio of European call and put options with weights inversely proportional to the square of strike. Care must, however, be taken with regard to the volatility smile as the wings (the deep in and out of the money option prices) can have a disproportionate effect on the price.

A volatility smile model is needed to correctly price variance swaps. If we use the Heston model, a closed-form solution can be derived for the fair variance swap rate. We can derive the payoff of a variance swap using Ito's Lemma. We first assume that the underlying stock behavior is described as follows:

$$\frac{dS_t}{S_t} = \mu dt + \sigma dZ_t$$

Applying Ito's formula we get

$$d(\log S_t) = \left(\mu - \frac{\sigma^2}{2} \right) dt + \sigma dZ_t$$

$$\frac{dS_t}{S_t} - d(\log S_t) = \frac{\sigma^2}{2} dt$$

Taking integrals, the total variance is:

$$\text{Variance} = \frac{1}{T}\int_0^T \sigma^2 dt = \frac{2}{T}\left(\int_0^T \frac{dS_t}{S_t} - \ln\left(\frac{S_T}{S_0}\right)\right)$$

The total variance consists of a rebalanced hedge of $\frac{1}{S_t}$ and short a log contract.

Using a static replication argument, any twice continuously differentiable contract can be replicated using a bond, a future, and infinitely many puts and calls, we can show that a short log contract position is equal to being short a futures contract and a collection of puts and calls:

$$-\ln\left(\frac{S_T}{S^*}\right) = -\frac{S_T - S^*}{S^*} + \int_{K \leq S^*}(K - S_T)^+\frac{dK}{K^2} + \int_{K \geq S^*}(S_T - K)^+\frac{dK}{K^2}$$

Taking expectations and setting the value of the variance swap equal to zero, we can rearrange the formula to solve for the fair variance swap strike price:

$$K_{var} = \frac{2}{T}\left(rT - \left(\frac{S_0}{S^*}e^{rT} - 1\right) - \log\left(\frac{S^*}{S_0}\right) + e^{rT}\int_0^{S^*}\frac{1}{K^2}P(K)dK + e^{rT}\int_{S^*}^{\infty}\frac{1}{K^2}C(K)dK\right)$$

Where:

S_0 is the spot price of the underlying security

$S^* > 0$ is an arbitrary cutoff

K is the strike of each option in the collection of options used

Variance Swaps and the Credit Crunch

Before the financial crisis of 2007-2008, investment banks were willing to trade single stock variance swaps along with index variance swaps. Since the financial crisis, single-stock variance trading has significantly diminished. We believe this is because of the large losses sustained by many investment banks from these single-name exposures, dampening their appetites to continue participating in providing liquidity to this market, particularly on the short side. Post-financial crisis there has been an uptick in volatility swap trading based on demand from dispersion traders who require single-stock volatility exposures. The convexity of variance swaps and the fact that the static hedge no longer works if the underlying moves outside the range of initially available strikes made them unattractive from a risk management perspective.

Chapter 12 Questions

1. Why might an investor wish to trade a volatility swap instead of delta hedging an option?

2. What is the difference between volatility and variance? Why might a variance swap be easier to hedge than a volatility swap?

3. Suppose an investor bought a volatility swap with a notional of $100,000 and a strike price of $35. If realized volatility over the life of the swap was 42%, calculate the investor's approximate gain or loss.

4. How might a volatility swap be statically hedged? Explain.

5. Do variance swaps have convexity? How does this differ from volatility swaps?

6. How might the static hedge for a variance swap fail?

7. What is the usual the fair value of a variance swap at inception?

8. Are variance swaps cash settled or physically settled? Explain.

9. Do index dividends affect the value of a variance swap?

10. If an investor buys a one year variance swap on the S&P500, and the S&P500 rallies 40% that year, how might you expect that to affect the payoff of the swap? Explain.

11. Can variance swaps be statically hedged? What instruments are required in order to statically hedge a variance swap?

12. Why is a nonstandard calculation for variance used in variance swaps? What effects does this have on them?

13. Why did banks stop selling single stock variance swaps during the financial crisis of 2007-2008?

Chapter 13

MONTE CARLO METHODS

Monte Carlo methods are used in finance to value and analyze complex financial instruments by simulating the various sources of uncertainty affecting their value, and then determining their average value over a large range of resultant outcomes or paths. The Monte Carlo options pricing method was developed by Phelim Boyle in 1977. The Monte Carlo method for pricing options is often considered a method of last resort. The approach is particularly useful in the valuation of options with multiple sources of uncertainty or with complicated features, which would make them difficult or impossible to value through a Black–Scholes or lattice-based approach. The technique is widely used in valuing path-dependent structures like lookback and Asian options and in real options analysis. Historically, Monte Carlo methods were considered to be too slow to be competitive, but with the faster computing capability today, this constraint is much less of a concern.

The Monte Carlo Method

The Monte Carlo method involves simulating the underlying process followed by the various risk factors affecting the price of the derivative that we are trying to price. First you generate a price path for the underlying based upon the random movements of the various risk factors and calculate the payoff from the derivative based on that path (see Figure 13.1). Then you repeat these steps, generating numerous sample values of the payoff from the derivative in the future. Next you calculate the average of the sample payoffs giving an estimate of the derivative's expected payoff in a risk-neutral world. Finally you discount the payoff at the risk-free rate; this result is the fair value of the option today.

The number of iterations carried out is at the discretion of the operator, and depends on the required accuracy. It is usual to calculate the standard deviation of the discounted payoffs generated by the simulation. The uncertainty about the value of the derivative is inversely proportional to the square root of the number of iterations that you run.

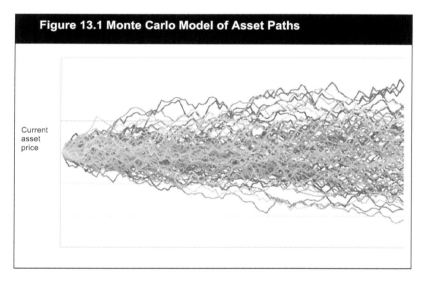

Figure 13.1 Monte Carlo Model of Asset Paths

Current asset price

Applying the Monte Carlo Method

The Monte Carlo method for pricing options can have great flexibility, complex stochastic processes (including jumps, mean reversion, or both) can be accommodated, and different distributions, including changing distributions can be assumed. The Monte Carlo method is generally used when there are three or more stochastic variables, which make using a PDE or lattice-based approach extremely difficult or impossible. Monte Carlo, in these situations can be more efficient than other approaches, as the time taken to run a Monte Carlo simulation increases in a linear manner with the number of variables, where for most other methods the time taken increases exponentially with the number of variables.

The Monte Carlo method is a brute force approach to pricing options, it does not rely on a lot of financial theory, it simply uses computer power to simulate thousands of possible paths for the underlying. The Monte Carlo method is by no means free of assumptions: you always assume a distribution for the driving asset, as well as structure for its volatility, and the absence of existence of jumps. The beauty of the Black-Scholes and lattice-based approaches is that they not only give you a fair value for the option, but they also specify a trading strategy, delta hedging, which allows you to hedge your risk exposures. Most of the options that require the Monte Carlo method to price are impossible to hedge. For this reason, the option is usually sold only when the buyer will pay well above fair value, as the seller usually has to keep that option on their books for its entire lifespan and can only roughly hedge it.

Advantages of the Monte Carlo method are that it can be used not only to price options where the payoff depends on the final price of the underlying on the expiration date, but also when the payoff depends on the price path followed by the underlying. The Monte Carlo method can similarly be used to value options where the payoff depends on the value of multiple underlying assets such as *basket options* or *rainbow options* (see Chapter 14 for discussion of these types of options). Here, correlation between asset returns is also incorporated.

The Monte Carlo method allows for a compounding in the uncertainty, such as where a joint probability distribution is used. In the case of only two random variables, this is called a *bivariate distribution*, but the concept generalizes to any number of random variables, giving a *multivariate distribution*. An example would be pricing an option on a stock in a foreign currency where the paths followed by the underlying stock and the exchange rate have to be modeled, but also the correlation between these two sources of risk must be incorporated.

The Monte Carlo method cannot easily handle situations where there are early exercise opportunities. In these situations, a Least Square Monte Carlo method, with a backward induction approach, is used.

The Monte Carlo Method and the Greeks

Calculating the Greeks using the Monte Carlo method is usually done by first pricing the derivative, and then recalculating the price of the derivative after making a small change in the input (such as spot price to calculate delta, or volatility if we are calculating vega) whose price sensitivity it is we are trying to find. The same number of iterations should be run in calculating the new price as were used when initially pricing the derivative.

Chapter 13 Questions

1. Is the Monte Carlo method always the best method for pricing options?

2. There are a number of assumptions underlying the Black-Scholes formula, are there any underlying the Monte Carlo method?

3. Would you expect the Binomial Tree approach or the Monte Carlo method to be more useful in pricing an American call option on an equity? Explain your choice.

4. How are the Greeks of an option calculated using the Monte Carlo method?

5. Do the number of iterations used in pricing an option using the Monte Carlo method matter?

Chapter 14

EXOTIC OPTIONS

Simple put and call options or combinations of them are called "vanilla" or plain vanilla options. These have standard properties and trade actively. The alternatives to these are called "exotic" options. Typically these are OTC and have various nonstandard features.

Exotics serve market niches including: specific hedging needs; tax, accounting, legal, or regulatory needs; or offer investors unique payoffs in particular market circumstances that are not easily accessible to Investors were these products not available.

Nonstandard features include: a hybrid of American- or European-style exercise capabilities; alternative payoffs or payoffs that do not depend precisely on one strike price; fixed payout options above a specified strike price; or those with a payoff based on the average performance of the underlying over the option's life.

What are Bermudan Options?

Bermudan options are a cross between American- and European-style options. They are named Bermudan options because Bermuda is physically between the U.S. and Europe. These options can be exercised on certain dates during the life of the option, often monthly. Bermudan options offer the sellers more control over when an option can be exercised against them, and therefore the contract is less expensive for the buyer than an American-style option, but not as inexpensive as a European option (which only allows exercise at expiration). These options can be priced using Binomial Trees where at particular nodes early exercise is a possibility, and at other nodes it is not.

What are Forward Start Options?

Forward start options are options that start at some point in the future; the exercise price is typically set at the current price at the beginning of the option's life. Employee stock options are an example of a forward start option. The other main purpose of trading them is to gain an exposure to forward volatility. Forward start options can be valued with a version of the Black-Scholes model (see Figure 14.1).

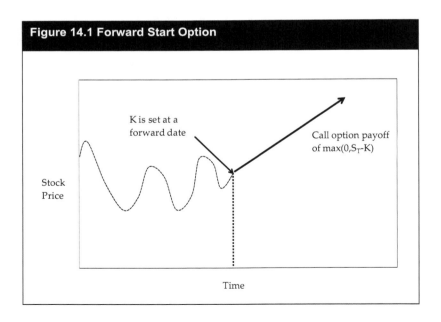

Figure 14.1 Forward Start Option

What are Compound Options?

Compound options are options on options: A call that enables you to buy another call, a put on a call, a call on a put, or a put on a put. The underlying asset of the first option is simply another option. Compound options allow buyers to effectively implement their strategy with greater leverage than one simple direct options position, and are cheaper at inception than a straight options position for the full timeframe. However because you make a second payment when you exercise the first option, the full amount of premiums paid on the two options will be greater than the premium on one option for the entire duration.

What are Chooser Options?

Chooser options allow the buyer, after a specified time, to choose if the option is a call or a put. This is particularly attractive if the underlying is expected to experience significant volatility, and potentially in *either* direction. This is riskier than a straddle strategy. With a chooser option, you might choose the call after it has rallied, but by the time expiry is approaching, the underlying may have fallen and you may end the contract out of the money, whereas with a straddle, you have a "live" put and a "live" call right up until maturity. As such, chooser options are cheaper than straddles.

What are Barrier Options?

Barrier option payoffs depend on whether the underlying hits a certain level, the barrier, before the expiration date. These options can either *knock-in* or *knock-out*. A knock-in option has no intrinsic value until the underlying touches the barrier price, at which point it becomes a vanilla option. A knock-out option is like a vanilla option but if the underlying exceeds the barrier price, it becomes worthless. There are eight types of barrier options: they can be up and out, or down and out calls or puts; or they can be down and in or up and in puts or calls (see Figure 14.2).

Barrier options are path-dependent options because their value depends on the previous prices of the underlying during the life of the option. Barrier options are always cheaper than an otherwise similar option without a barrier. As an example, if you were bullish on Facebook's stock over the next 1 year timeframe, but were confident that it would not exceed $250 per share over that period, you might be happy to buy a one year up and out call option with a strike around the current price ($150 at the time of writing this book) but a knock-out barrier at $250.

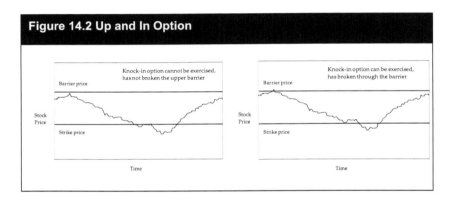

The Greeks on barrier options behave quite differently than those of vanilla options. If you compare an up-and-out call option with a vanilla call option. As the stock price moves up, a vanilla call will increase in value, while an up-and-out call is affected by two opposing forces. As the stock price moves up, the up-and-out call's payoff becomes potentially larger just like the vanilla call, but the upward move simultaneously threatens to destroy the value of the contract by moving it closer to the knock out barrier. This conflict makes the option value very sensitive to the stock's movement as it gets close to the barrier, and delta can flip rapidly from positive to negative at these points making these options very difficult to hedge. Barrier option values can decrease with increasing volatility, unlike vanilla calls and puts. The up-and-out call described above becomes more likely to get knocked out near the barrier as volatility increases. Even though the Investor is long volatility relative to the strike level, they are short volatility relative to the barrier.

What are Binary Options?

Binary options (also known as digital options) are discontinuous payoff options. An example would be a payoff of X if $S_T > K$, otherwise 0. So the owner of a binary call option would receive either a 0 payoff or a full, set payoff amount if the underlying's price is above a pre-set level K, but the payoff does not rise if the underlying is well above the strike K, instead it is a fixed payoff of X (see Figure 14.3). These are difficult for dealers to hedge well, particularly when the underlying trades close to the strike near maturity.

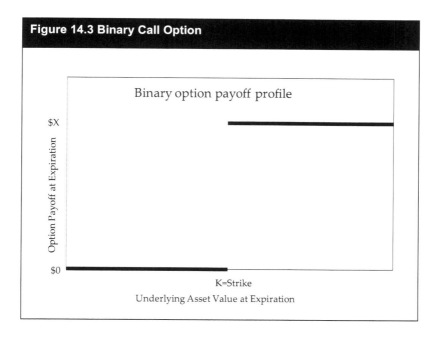

Figure 14.3 Binary Call Option

Binary option payoff profile

$X

$0

Option Payoff at Expiration

K=Strike

Underlying Asset Value at Expiration

What are Gap Options?

A *gap option* is a type of barrier option where the strike making the option exercisable differs from the strike used to calculate the payoff. Gap call options payoff $S_T - K_1$ when S_T is greater than K_2. A modified Black-Scholes formula can be used to price this style of option.

What are Lookback Options?

Lookback option payoffs depend on maximums or minimums of underlying asset price points over the option's life. These are path-dependent options that allow the option owners to "buy at the low" or "sell at the high" over the life of the option. The life of the option being from the contract first being agreed upon through to the expiration date. There are two types of lookback options: floating-strike and fixed-strike.

For *floating-strike lookback calls*, the exercise price is the minimum stock price reached over the life of the option. For *floating-strike lookback puts*, the exercise price is the maximum stock price reached over the life of the option.

For *fixed-strike* options, the strike is fixed as with a vanilla option but, for *fixed-strike lookback calls* the owner gets to exercise at the point when the underlying asset price is at its highest level over the life of the option. For *fixed-strike lookback puts*, the owner gets to exercise at the underlying asset's lowest price over the life of the option.

While these options sound like you cannot lose with them, they are of course priced in a rational market and are considerably more expensive than vanilla options. Their high prices can be reduced by restricting the maximums and minimums used in calculating the payoffs, and these restricted versions are known as *partial lookback options*.

What are Asian Options?

Asian option payoffs depend on the average price of the underlying over the option's life, or some part of the option's life, rather than the spot price of the underlying on the expiration date. The average can be calculated as either a geometric or arithmetic average. The primary advantage of Asian options is that they reduce the potential for singular episodes of market manipulation or one-off unusual price moves to undermine your investment thesis, which might have otherwise been accurate. Because of the volatility-dampening effect of the averaging feature, these are also cheaper than European or American options.

What are Rainbow Options?

Rainbow options are those where delivery at maturity can be on a choice of a number of assets. These are usually calls or puts on a best-of or worst-of a basket of Y underlying assets. This is also considered a type of correlation trading because the prices of these options are sensitive to the correlation among the basket's constituents. Often Monte Carlo methods are used to value rainbow options.

What are Basket Options?

Basket options have payoffs that depend on the performance of a basket of assets such as a set of individual stocks or indices, or a group of currencies. Typically the owner of a basket option has the right, but not the obligation, to buy or sell a basket of underlying assets at maturity. These are commonly used for currency hedging in institutions with varied currency exposures, and often end up being cheaper than individual options purchased on each currency.

What are Quantos?

Quantity-adjusting options or *quantos* are derivatives where the underlying is denominated in a currency other than that in which the option is settled. A quanto has an embedded currency forward with a variable notional amount. They are attractive to investors who wish to have exposure to a foreign asset, but without the corresponding foreign exchange risk. These are used when investors expect the underlying foreign asset to perform well but do not expect that the foreign country's currency will perform well over the same timeframe. Quanto futures, quanto options, and quanto swaps are available.

What are Weather Derivatives?

Many companies' economic performance depend heavily on the weather, for example farming, tourism, electricity generation, natural gas production, or outdoor-event organizing. *Weather derivatives* provide payoffs to those who seek to speculate or hedge their risks around weather events. Power companies may use heating degree days (HDD) or cooling degree days (CDD) contracts to smooth earnings. An outdoor-event management company could enter into a weather derivative contract that would pay off if it rains on the day of a sporting event they are organizing. These are considered exotic options given that the underlying assets cannot be directly valued in pricing the derivatives.

What are Energy Derivatives

Energy derivatives are important for companies to manage their costs and production exposures. Crude oil is the largest global commodity market. Electricity markets are unique in terms of commodities derivatives markets since electricity cannot easily be stored. Capacity, supply and demand, weather, and timing are extremely complex for electricity derivatives. Historically, oil market volatility is often 20% annualized, natural gas volatility is 40% annualized, and electricity markets often exhibit 100%–200% volatility per annum.

What are Insurance Derivatives?

Insurance companies sometimes hedge themselves against extremely expensive catastrophes through what is called "reinsurance." *Insurance derivatives* base their value on an underlying insurance-related statistic. For example, an insurance derivative could offer a payout to its owner if a specific index of hurricane losses exceeded a specified level.

Chapter 14 Questions

1. What is the difference between exotic options and vanilla options? Which type is more popular with investors?

2. Are exotic options usually exchange traded?

3. How do Bermudan options differ from American options? All other things equal, should Bermudan options cost more or less than American options? Why?

4. What is a compound option? Why might people wish to trade them?

5. How does a chooser option differ from a straddle? How does it differ from a strangle?

6. Explain how a down-and-in call option might work.

7. What is a gap option? Draw the payoff profile of a gap call option.

8. Typically, would you expect a call option to cost more or less than a lookback call? Explain your reasoning.

9. What is the difference between a floating-strike and a fixed-strike lookback call option?

10. List the eight types of standard barrier options.

11. How do Asian options differ from European options? Which would you usually expect to be more expensive all other things equal?

12. Name three types of path-dependent exotic options.

13. In 2013, economists were anticipating that huge financial stimulus in Japan would drive up Japanese stock markets, but possibly with detrimental effects to the Japanese currency, the

Yen. What type of exotic could a trader enter into to profit from a rise in foreign stock prices without being exposed to foreign exchange movements?

14. How might insurance derivatives work on hurricane reinsurance in Florida? Explain the type of structure you'd expect to see.

Chapter 15

INTEREST RATES & FINANCIAL SWAPS

Interest Rates

An *interest rate* is the rate at which interest is paid by borrowers for the use of money that they borrow from lenders, usually expressed as a percentage of principal. Interest rates are typically noted on an annual basis, known as the *annual percentage rate* (APR). The assets borrowed could be cash or goods.

Interest rates factor into all economic decisions and all derivatives. The interest rate charged typically depends on the credit risk of borrower: the greater the credit risk, the higher the interest rate charged. The most fundamental concept in finance is the idea of discounting future cash flows at an interest rate.

In any given currency a variety of interest rates exist. The most important rates for the purposes of this book are sovereign rates, LIBOR rates and repo rates.

Sovereign Bond Rates

The *sovereign rate* is the rate of interest relating to borrowing by a government in its own currency. In the United States this is referred to as the Treasury rate. It is usually assumed that a government will not default on a loan in its own currency, as it can simply print currency to pay it back. For this reason, the sovereign rate is regarded as the risk-free rate in a given country.

What is LIBOR?

LIBOR stands for the London Interbank Offered Rate which is the interest rate at which large international banks lend to each other. It is the primary benchmark for short-term interest rates around the world. *LIBOR rates* are calculated for five currencies and seven borrowing periods ranging from overnight to one year. The rates are published each business day. LIBOR is a high grade institutional rate, it is typically higher than sovereign rates since it is not risk free. Many financial institutions set their own interest rates relative to it. Over $350 trillion of derivatives and other financial products are tied to LIBOR interest rates.

What are Repurchase Agreements?

Repos are short-term agreements to sell securities to a counterparty and repurchase them at a slightly higher pre-agreed price. It amounts to a type of short-term collateralized loan, where the high-grade securities are retained as collateral. The term *repo rate* usually refers to the cost of overnight borrowing or "overnight repo" interest. Longer term collateralized borrowing arrangements are referred to as "term repo." The repo rate is usually only slightly higher that the sovereign rate due to its extremely low credit risk, as the collateral posted generally makes the transaction very safe from the lender's point of view.

Zero Coupon Interest Rates

A zero-coupon bond is a bond bought at a price below its face value (assuming a positive time value of money). There are no periodic interest payments, or "coupons," hence the term zero-coupon bond. When the bond matures, its investor receives its face value in full. Examples of zero-coupon bonds include US Treasury bills, US savings bonds, or Treasury STRIPS (Separate Trading of Registered Interest and Principal of Securities). *Bootstrapping* is a method for constructing a zero-coupon yield curve from the prices of a group of coupon-bearing bonds (see Example later in this chapter).

The Risk-Free Rate

The *risk-free rate* is the interest rate an investor would expect from an absolutely risk-free investment over a specified period of time. Technically there is no such thing as a risk-free rate given that there is no such thing as a return without risk; however, most sovereign rates are called risk-free as their obligations are in the same currency that the governments are able to print their own currency in, and the government is able to raise revenues in its own country, thereby making the risk of default so low as to be negligible.

Bond Prices vs. Interest Rates

As interest rates increase, bond prices fall, and vice-versa, as interest rates decline, bond prices rise (see Figure 15.1).

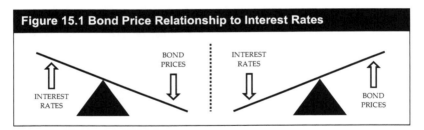

Figure 15.1 Bond Price Relationship to Interest Rates

What is a Credit Spread?

A *credit spread* is the difference in yield between different fixed income securities, brought about by different credit quality. The credit spread is the additional net yield an investor requires in order to invest in a security with credit risk relative to one with no credit risk. The credit spread of a risky security is usually quoted in relation to the yield on a credit risk-free benchmark security or *reference rate*. There are several measures of credit spread, including Z-spread and option-adjusted spread.

Compounding Reminder

Putting $100 in a bank account at a 5% interest rate will compound as follows:

Annually	=	$100 (1 + 0.05)	=	$105
Semi-annually	=	$100(1+0.025)(1.025)	=	$105.06
Quarterly	=	$100(1+0.0125)^4	=	$105.09
Continuously	=	$100(e^r)$	=	$105.13

Implied Zero Coupon Interest Rates

The value of a bond is the present value of all of its cash flows, each discounted at their annualized "zero coupon" discount rate. If we have a bond with three remaining payments, two semi-annual interest payments and one final payment of principal and interest, it is valued as follows:

$$\text{Bond price} = \text{Interest}_{n-2} \cdot e^{(-r_{0.5} \cdot 0.5)} + \text{Interest}_{n-1} \cdot e^{(-r_1 \cdot 1)} + (\text{Principal} + \text{Interest}_n) \cdot e^{(-r_{1.5} \cdot 1.5)}$$

Bootstrapping

Suppose we want to know the appropriate 1.5 year zero-coupon discount rate. If we know that the 0.5 year spot rate is 2.5%, the one year spot rate is 2.8% (we get these rates from T bills, which are zero coupon). We can then use these rates to calculate the 1.5 year spot rate if we know the 1.5 year coupon bond's price and coupon. Suppose the 1.5 year coupon bond is selling at par, with a coupon of 3.1%, paid semi-annually. This means that every 6 months, prior to maturity, the bondholder receives 100*3.1%/2, which is a 1.55 cash flow. Then at maturity, the bondholder receives that 1.55 cash flow, plus the principal amount of 100. We can solve for r_3, the 1.5

year spot rate by backing it out of the formula below:

$$100 = \frac{1.55}{(1 + 2.5\%/2)} + \frac{1.55}{(1 + 2.8\%/2)^2} + \frac{101.55}{(1 + r_3/2)^3}$$

Solving for r3 in the formula above, we get that the 1.5 year zero coupon bond equals 3.1063%.

Forward Interest Rates

A forward rate is an interest rate implied for periods of time in the future by zero-coupon bonds. For example, the market implied yield on a three-month Treasury bill three months from now is a forward rate.

If we know what the three-month zero-coupon Treasury bill rate is and what the six-month zero-coupon Treasury bill rate is, we can back out what the market is implying as the yield on a three-month Treasury bill three months from now.

To calculate forward rates we just need the zero-coupon yield curve. The formulas are as follows:

Simple rate:

$$r_{t_1,t_2} = \frac{1}{d_2 - d_1} \left(\frac{1 + r_2 d_2}{1 + r_1 d_1} - 1 \right)$$

Compound rate:

$$r_{t_1,t_2} = \left(\frac{(1 + r_2)^{d_2}}{(1 + r_1)^{d_1}} \right)^{\frac{1}{d_2 - d_1}} - 1$$

Exponential rate:

$$r_{t_1,t_2} = \frac{r_2 d_2 - r_1 d_1}{d_2 - d_1}$$

$r_{t1,t2}$ is the forward rate between term t_1 and term t_2

d_1 is the time length between time 0 and term t_1 (in years)
d_2 is the time length between time 0 and term t_2 (in years)
r_1 is the zero-coupon yield for the time period $(0,t_1)$
r_2 is the zero-coupon yield for the time period $(0,t_2)$

Forward Rate Calculation

Suppose you have a 2 year loan at 3% such that $100 \times e^{(3\% \times 2)}$ = $106.18. This could be expressed precisely by each year's separate rates: year one cost of 2.4% and year 2 with a cost of 3.6%. These give the same result of $100 \times e^{(2.4\% \times 1)} \times e^{(3.6\% \times 1)}$ = $106.18.

R_1 is 2.4%, R_2 is 3%, and R_F for a forward starting loan beginning at the end of year 1 and ending at the end of year 2 is 3.6%.

What is an FRA?

A *forward rate agreement* (FRA) is an over-the-counter agreement to borrow a fixed amount of money at a fixed interest rate at a specified future time period.

Banks and large corporations can use FRAs to hedge future interest rate exposures. The buyer hedges against the risk of rising interest rates, while the seller hedges against the risk of falling interest rates. Speculators can use FRAs to make bets on future changes in interest rates.

Rates in the future will usually be different from the implied rate at the time you entered into a forward-rate-agreement, giving rise to gains or losses on the agreed transaction.

Forward Rate Gains / Losses Example

Suppose you agree to lend $100 million for a six month timeframe, starting in 2 years, to earn a 3.5% return.

Two years passes, and it turns out that the market rate for the next six months is 4%. This means you have a loss on your original trade. Your cash flows will then be, at the end of the 2.5 years: $100m(3.5% − 4%) × 0.5 = −$250,000. (Interest rates in FRAs are expressed in non-continuous compounding.)

What are Financial Swaps?

A *swap* is a derivative in which two counterparties exchange the cash flow for one party's financial instrument for those of the other party's financial instrument for a period of time stated in the agreement These cash flow streams are known as "the legs" of the swap. The swap agreement defines the dates when the cash flows are to be paid and how they are calculated. The cash flows are calculated over a notional principal amount. The notional amount is usually not exchanged between counterparties—it is just used as a reference from which the size of the two payment streams can be calculated.

Usually at the swap's inception, at least one of the cash flows is an uncertain variable; for example, a floating interest rate. The change in value for the uncertain cash flow will benefit one of the two parties financially. However, both parties may benefit overall, if not financially, by reducing financial uncertainty as explained in chapter 2 - Should Companies Hedge?. The first swap was negotiated in 1981 when IBM and World Bank entered into a swap agreement. Since then swaps have become one of the most heavily traded types of derivatives in the world.

Interest rate swaps can be most easily understood as an exchange of loans. Consider two parties that have taken out loans of equal value. The first has borrowed at a fixed rate and the other at a floating rate. Both would like to balance their portfolio to limit risk. The two then agree to exchange their loans, or swap interest rates. They are likely doing this as a hedge, to reduce their overall interest rate risk, or to speculate on the future direction of interest rates. The principal amount of the two loans is the same, thus there is no need to exchange principal, leaving only the quarterly cash flows to be exchanged. The party that switches to paying a floating rate might request a premium or offer a discount on the original fixed borrower's rate, depending on how interest rate expectations have changed since the inception of the original loans. The original fixed rate, plus the premium or minus the discount, would be the equivalent of a swap rate.

Hedging With Swaps

The normal commercial operations of many businesses lead to risks associated with interest rates or foreign exchange. Consider a US savings and loan association. Savings and loans accept deposits and pay a floating rate of interest on them. They then lend those deposits out as home mortgages. In the United States, home mortgages are typically fixed interest rate loans as opposed to the floating rate loans in the United Kingdom. As a result, a US-based savings and loan bank can be left with fixed-rate assets and floating-rate liabilities. This would lead to losses in a rising interest rate environment. To escape this interest rate risk, the savings and loan bank could use the swaps market to convert either their liabilities to fixed rate, or their assets to floating rate. Initially, interest rate swaps helped corporations manage their interest rate risk exposures. However, because swaps reflect the market's expectations for interest rates in the future, swaps also became an attractive tool for other fixed-income market participants, including investors, speculators, and banks.

What is an ISDA Agreement?

The ISDA Master Agreement is a legal document published by the International Swaps and Derivatives Association, ("ISDA") which is used to provide certain legal and credit protection for parties who enter into over-the-counter derivatives. The agreement sets out standard terms that apply to all of the transactions entered into between the parties of the agreement, thus, each time a transaction is entered into, the terms of the master agreement do not need to be re-negotiated, they apply automatically.

In addition to the Master Agreement text which is standardized, there is a Schedule which allows parties to add to or amend the standard terms. The Schedule is what negotiators negotiate, and this can take some time for the parties to agree upon.

When parties enter into an OTC derivatives transaction a Confirmation is prepared detailing the terms of that specific trade. Each Confirmation will reference the ISDA Master Agreement and the trade is then covered by the terms of the Agreement. The ISDA Master Agreement is a netting agreement where all of the Transactions depend upon each other. A default on one transaction counts as a default on all transactions.

ISDA produces detailed supporting materials for the Master Agreement, including definitions and user's guides. These supporting materials are designed to prevent disputes and to facilitate the consistent use and interpretation of the Master Agreement. These materials are regularly updated to reflect the current regulatory and market environments.

It would be extremely difficult for an individual investor to meet the standards required to enter into an ISDA agreement, and for this reason Swaps are not usually available to retail investors. Typically swaps are transacted in by banks, insurance companies, large corporates, Institutional investors and governments.

What is a Plain Vanilla Swap

The term *plain vanilla* when used in finance usually signifies the most basic or standard version of a financial instrument. Plain vanilla is the opposite of an exotic instrument, which is a term used to describe a more complex security.

The most common type of swap is known as a "plain vanilla" interest rate swap which involves one counterparty paying a fixed rate to another counterparty while receiving a floating rate indexed to a reference rate like LIBOR in return. By market convention, the counterparty paying the fixed rate is the "payer," and the counterparty receiving the fixed rate is the "receiver" (see Figure 15.2).

The notional principal is an amount used as a basis for calculations, but is not actually transferred between the two counterparties. If, for example, the notional principal is $1 million, this then allows us to calculate the amount of the payments based on the two interest rates.

For each exchange, the floating rate is set at the beginning of the period and paid at the end of the period.

In order for a swap to be valued at zero at inception, the present value of the two legs of the swap must be equal. If you calculate the net present value of the two cash flows, the correct fixed rate is the one at which the two cash flows have an equal present value.

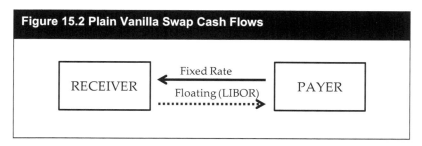

Figure 15.2 Plain Vanilla Swap Cash Flows

A Swap Example

Suppose ABC and XYZ agree to an interest rate swap. ABC agrees to pay a fixed rate at 4% and XYZ agrees to pay a floating rate at LIBOR. The notional principal is $100 million, payments are semi-annual, and the maturity is three years (see Figure 15.3).

At the outset, we don't know who will "win" since we don't know the path that LIBOR rates will actually take in the markets. We do know that there are six cash flow exchanges and that at each point ABC will pay XYZ $2 million.

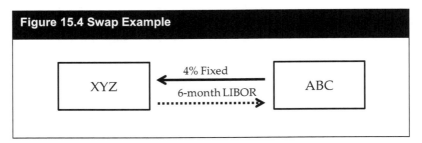

Figure 15.4 Swap Example

Assume now that three years has passed, Table 15.1 shows how the swap works out.

Note that the notional principal, in this example $100 million, does not change hands at any point between the two parties (it would make no sense for them to wire each other an identical amount of money at the outset), it is just the figure upon which the individual interest calculations are based.

Table 15.1 ABC"s Realized Cash Flows

Payment Period	Realized LIBOR Rates	Floating CFs Received	Fixed CFs Paid	Net CFs Exchanged
Period 1	3.2%	=100m x (3.2%/ 2) = 1.6m	2m	-0.40m
Period 2	3.7%	1.85m	2m	-0.15m
Period 3	4.2%	2.10m	2m	0.10m
Period 4	4.4%	2.20m	2m	0.20m
Period 5	4.5%	2.25m	2m	0.25m
Period 6	4.8%	2.40m	2m	0.4m

Note that the interest rate swap allows the counterparties to do the same thing as the savings and loan bank mentioned earlier, that is, to change borrowings from fixed to floating or vice-versa. In the example, ABC switched its borrowing from floating to fixed, believing rates would rise, and XYZ switched its borrowing from fixed to floating, believing rates would fall.

The Market for Interest Rate Swaps

A significant industry has grown in order to facilitate swap transactions. Initially, investment banks would match counterparties and charge them a fee. Over time they moved to a model where they "make markets" in interest rate swaps, and charge a "spread." The spread charged compensates the dealer for the risk of counterparty default, the risk of mismatched entry timing to each 'leg,' and provides a profit. Dealers usually have a portfolio of swaps to manage and can find themselves exposed to the very risks their customers are trying to avoid.

There are many customers who transact in swaps.

Swap brokers serve as information intermediaries; they have a number of potential counterparties in their contact list and stand ready to find a suitable counterparty for a swap upon demand. The broker will protect the identity of the interested parties until they have found a very likely counterparty. For their services, a swap broker receives a fee from each of the counterparties.

Swap dealers serve as financial intermediaries and fulfill all of the roles of the swap broker, but they may also take risk positions in swap transactions by becoming an actual party to the transaction. Usually the swap dealer will take a risk position in order to facilitate the trade of the initial customer, but they will quickly seek to offset that risk in the market. The swap dealer will charge a spread as shown in Figure 15.4.

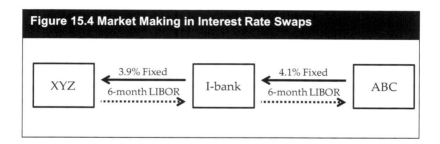

Figure 15.4 Market Making in Interest Rate Swaps

Most swaps are traded over-the-counter, but some types of swaps are also traded on exchanges such as the Chicago Mercantile Exchange, the Chicago Board Options Exchange, the Intercontinental Exchange, and Eurex AG.

Who Trades Swaps?

Company treasurers: Companies can set up swaps to hedge their interest rate exposure or to more closely match their assets or income stream as explained above.

Speculators: Swaps give fixed-income traders a way to speculate on movements in interest rates while reducing the cost of long and short positions in Treasuries. Instead of buying a Treasury bond to speculate on a fall in interest rates, a trader could "receive" fixed in a swap, which gives a similar payoff should rates fall, but does not require the investor to put up as much capital.

Portfolio managers: Interest rate swaps give fixed-income portfolio managers the ability to quickly add or reduce the duration of their portfolio. They give portfolio managers a way of adjusting interest rate exposure and offsetting the risks posed by interest rate volatility. Long-dated interest rate swaps can be an effective tool in *liability driven investing*, allowing portfolio managers to increase the duration of a portfolio, where the aim is to match the duration of assets with that of long-term liabilities.

Risk managers: Financial institutions are usually involved in a huge number of transactions involving loans, derivatives contracts, and other investments all of which can expose the institution to interest rate risk. This risk can be managed using swaps.

Bond issuers: When corporations decide to issue bonds, they usually lock in an interest rate by entering into swap contracts. That gives them time to go out and find investors for the bonds. Once the bonds are sold, they can exit the swap contracts. The swap contracts will have hedged the interest rate risk between the sales pitch forthe bonds and the actual sale.

The History of Swaps

Currency swaps originated in the late 1970s when foreign exchange traders entered these agreements to work around British controls on the movement of foreign currency. The first interest rate swap was negotiated in 1981 between the World Bank and IBM. IBM at that time had large amounts of Swiss franc and German deutschemark debt. IBM and the World Bank worked out an arrangement in which the World Bank borrowed dollars in the US market and swapped the dollar payment obligation to IBM in exchange for taking over IBM's Swiss franc and deutschemark obligations. The swap market has grown immensely since then, the notional dollar value of outstanding interest rate swaps globally was $318 trillion at the end of 2017 according to the Bank for International Settlements.

The swaps market gave rise to ISDA (the International Swaps and Derivatives Association), the global trade association that created the core documentation for the over-the-counter derivatives world.

Swaps are easily the largest part of the derivatives world by notional values outstanding.

Swaps and the Law of Comparative Advantage

In economics, the law of absolute advantage stated that countries should specialize in what they are best or most efficient at producing, and then exchange these goods with other countries, making both countries better off.

David Ricardo's vital contribution to economic thought was the law of *comparative advantage*, an economic theory stating that even if one country is more efficient in the production of all goods (absolute advantage in all goods) than the other, both countries will still gain by trading with each other, as long as they have different relative efficiencies. This law helps explain why countries engage in international trade even when one country's workers are more efficient at producing every single good than workers in other countries.

It is easy to understand how if one company is able to get a better deal in fixed-rate borrowing, but prefers to borrow at a floating rate, while another company is in the equal and opposite situation, it might make sense for these two companies to enter into a swap. In the situation where one firm has better access to the capital markets than all others, it might still make sense for them to enter the swaps market.

Borrowing capabilities in the market:

Company X can borrow at 3.5% fixed or LIBOR–0.2% floating.

Company Y can borrow at 4.5% fixed or LIBOR+0.4% floating.

Company X can borrow fixed at a 1% better rate than Company Y, but only 0.6% better on a floating basis than Company Y. Company X has a comparative advantage in the fixed borrowing markets.

If Company X prefers to borrow floating, and Company Y prefers to borrow fixed, they can enter into a swap agreement with each other and improve both of their borrowing costs.

The fixed advantage of 1% minus the floating advantage of 0.6% = 0.4% which can be split evenly between the two counterparties.

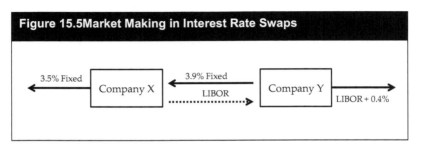

Figure 15.5Market Making in Interest Rate Swaps

Cash flows to Company X are: −3.5%+3.9%−LIBOR, meaning they end up with a floating cost of borrow rate of LIBOR−0.4% which is 0.20% better than they could have otherwise achieved in the floating rate loans marketplace.

Cash flows to Company Y are: +LIBOR−3.9%−(LIBOR+0.4%), meaning they end up with a fixed cost of borrow rate of 4.3%, which is 0.20% better than they could have otherwise achieved in the fixed-rate borrowing marketplace (see Figure 15.5).

While the above example is used frequently in derivatives textbooks, we would point out that it does have flaws. The reason that Company Y had an absolute disadvantage in borrowing in both fixed and floating rate markets is most likely due to Y having a higher default risk than X. Should this not be the case, you would expect the difference to have been arbitraged away years ago due to the existence of the swaps market. While X may still wish to enter into this transaction, the risk they are taking on in order to reduce their borrowing cost most likely relates to taking on counterparty risk.

Pricing Interest Rate Swaps

As explained above, swaps are typically valued at zero at inception. Afterward they, may take on a positive or negative valuation. Swaps are a zero-sum game, one counterparty's gain is equal to the other counterparty's loss.

If you receive fixed:

Swap value = present value of fixed cash-flows − present value of floating cash-flows

If you pay fixed:

Swap value = present value of floating cash-flows − present value of fixed cash-flows

A plain vanilla interest rate swap can be priced as either a combination of a long position in one bond and a short position in another bond, or as a portfolio of forward-rate-agreements. All discounting is done using LIBOR zero-coupon interest rates, as it is assumed that the risk on the cash flows is equivalent to a loan in the interbank market.

Example: Pricing an Interest Rate Swap

Suppose that a swap has been in existence for some time already and that we now are looking to value it. Assume that it pays floating 6 month LIBOR versus 5% fixed, semi-annually. It is on a $100 million notional and has 1.75 years remaining. Suppose we know that LIBOR continuously compounded is 6%, 6.5%, 7%, and 7.3% for the 3 month, 9 month, 15 month and 21 month periods. We are also aware that the last payment date 6-month LIBOR price was 6.2%. What is the value of this swap?

There are two methods to do this calculation. One calculates the equivalent bond values, one fixed, one floating, and takes the difference between these present values. The other method involves calculating the FRAs for each of the upcoming payment periods, and then taking the present value of the differences in fixed/floating cash flows from each upcoming payment period.

Table 15.2Swap Valuation - Bond Method

Payment Period	Fixed Bond CFs	Floating Bond Value	Discount Factor	Present Value Fixed Bond	Present Value Floating Bond
3 months	2.5m	$=100m+100m \times (6.2\%/\ 2)=103.1m$	$=e^{(-6\%\times3/\ 12)}=0.9851$	2.4628m	101.5650m
9 months	2.5m		0.9524	2.3810m	
15 months	2.5m		0.9162	2.2905m	
21 months	102.5m		0.8801	90.2075m	
Total				$97.3419m	$101.5650m

Table 15.2 shows the calculations of the bond valuation method for our example. The value to the "receive fixed" counterparty is the Fixed Bond valuation minus the Floating Bond valuation, therefore

the swap is worth -\$4.22 million. The opposing counterparty has the opposite value.

Figure 15.3 Swap Valuation - FRA Method

Time	Fixed CFs	FRA continuously compounded	FRA Semi-ann	Floating CFs	Discount Factor	PV Net CFs
3 m	2.5m		6.2%	-\$3.1m	0.9851	-.59107m
9 m	2.5m	$=(6.5\% \cdot 0.75 - 6\% \cdot 0.25)/\ 0.5 = 6.75\%$	$=2\sqrt{e^{6.75\%}}-1)=6.87\%$	-3.4326m	0.9524	-.8882m
15 m	2.5m	7.75%	7.9%	-3.9511m	0.9162	-1.3294m
21 m	2.5m	8.05%	8.21%	-4.1071m	0.8801	-1.4144m
Total						**-\$4.2232m**

Table 15.3 shows the swap valuation using the FRA method to be -\$4.22 million, the same as the bond method.

Foreign Exchange Swaps

A *foreign exchange swap* is an over-the-counter currency derivative between two institutions to exchange the principal and/or interest payments of a loan in one currency for equivalent amounts, in net present value terms, in another currency. A currency swap differs from an interest rate swap in that both principal and interest of the loan are exchanged. While in an interest rate swap, there is no reason for the counterparties to wire each other the identical notional amount, it does make sense in a currency swap, because the sum of money is denominated in two different currencies. The principal amounts are exchanged at the beginning and again at the end of the life of the swap. The principal amounts are typically chosen to be equal given the exchange rate at swap initiation so that the valuation at inception is zero.

The purpose of a foreign exchange swap is to transform the borrowing currencies of the counterparties.

Foreign Exchange Swap Example

Table 15.4 shows an example of a four-year agreement between

USAco and BRITco where USAco pays fixed 3% GBP, and receives fixed 4% USD. They each make one interest payment per year, and the principal amounts are $15.2 million and £10 million. This is a fixed-for-fixed currency swap.

Table 15.4 Fixed-for-Fixed Currency Swap, USAco's cash flows

Payment Period	USD	GBP
Year 0	-$15.2m	+£10m
Year 1	+0.61m	-£0.3m
Year 2	+0.61m	-£0.3m
Year 3	+0.61m	-£0.3m
Year 4	+15.81m	-£10.3m

Pricing Foreign Exchange Swaps

Fixed-for-fixed foreign exchange swaps can be broken down into a position in two bonds, as with the interest rate swap, or into a series of forward contracts.

Looking at the bond valuation method, the value of the swap is as follows:

Local Currency received:

Swap Value = bond value with domestic flows – spot exchange rate (foreign price bond with foreign flows)

Foreign Currency received:

Swap Value = spot exchange rate (foreign price bond with foreign flows) – bond value with domestic flows

What are Dividend Swaps?

Dividend swaps originated in the early 2000s. They came about due to the popularity of structured products such as equity-linked notes which became popular in the 1990s. Most equity-linked notes reflect capital appreciation alone and do not include gains from dividends and dividend reinvestment for tax reasons. Investment banks were thus left holding streams of potentially volatile dividend payments which they wished to hedge their exposure to, giving rise to the dividend swap.

A *dividend swap* is an over-the-counter derivative where the holder of the fixed leg pays the other party a pre-designated fixed payment at each interval in exchange for the total dividends that were paid out by a selected underlying. The underlying can be a single company, a basket of companies, or all the members of an index. The payments are multiplied by a notional number of shares.

Like most swaps, the contract is usually arranged so that its value at signing is zero. This is accomplished by making the value of the fixed leg equal to the value of the floating leg. Thus, the fixed leg will be set at the average expected dividends over the term of the swap for the given underlying.

Dividend swaps share some risk similarity to an investment in cash equities, as both involve exchanging a fixed amount of money for a set of uncertain future dividends. A cash equity investment however has a much higher dividend duration than the dividend swap in the same way that a perpetuity has a higher interest rate duration[9] than a fixed maturity bond.

Other Types of Swap

There are numerous variations available on the plain vanilla swap

---

[9] Duration is a measure of the sensitivity of the price of a fixed-income investment to a change in interest rates.

structure that are limited only by the imagination and interest of market participants. Well known examples are:

Commodity swaps, where a floating (or spot) price based on an underlying commodity is exchanged for a fixed price over a specified period. No commodities are exchanged during the trade.

Equity swaps, where the dividends and capital gains realized on an equity or equity index are exchanged for either a fixed or floating interest rate.

Variance and volatility swaps, which have their own chapter in this book.

Zero coupon swaps, which are of use to corporations who have floating rate liabilities but would like to conserve cash for operational purposes.

Interest rate swaps can be arranged on non-LIBOR rates. Currency swaps can be fixed-for-floating which are known as cross-currency interest rate swaps, or floating-for-floating. Principal amounts can reduce over time (amortize) or increase over time (step-up swaps). Sometimes options are embedded in swaps making them extendable, callable, or puttable. *Swaptions* are an option giving the right but not the obligation to engage in a swap.

Credit Risk with Interest Rate Swaps

Because swaps are over-the-counter private transactions between institutions, they have credit risk, which is known in the swaps market as counterparty risk.

Swaps are usually valued at zero at inception, and as time goes by, the swap will take on a value based on movements in the underlying markets. Let us refer to the counterparty who is ahead in the trade half way through the life of the swap as the "winning" party, and the counterparty who is down as the "losing" party. If the losing party goes bankrupt, this will lead to a credit loss for the winning party. Assuming that no recovery is possible, the total loss will be the present value of the net interest payments remaining. This is known as the replacement cost of the swap, and is a commonly used measure of credit loss. Conversely, if the winning party happens to go bankrupt during the life of a swap, the losing party does not get to walk away from the contract. For this reason, the replacement cost is the greater of the fair market value of the contract and zero. This is known as *current credit exposure*. Potential losses from defaults on a swap are much less than losses from default on a loan of the same size, as the value of a swap is usually only a fraction of the value of a loan.

In recent years, since the financial crisis of 2007-2008, counterparty credit risk has emerged as an increasingly important factor in financial markets. Concerns about counterparty credit risk were significantly heightened in early 2008 by the collapse of Bear Stearns, and skyrocketed later that year when Lehman Brothers declared Chapter 11 bankruptcy and defaulted on its debt and swap obligations. In the wake of this financial crisis and as part of the Dodd-Frank financial regulatory reform plan of 2009, pressure has been placed on traders of derivatives such as swaps to make their trades on an open exchange with a clearing house. The Dodd-Frank Act mandates that all routine derivatives be traded on Swap Execution Facilities (SEFs) or exchanges and be cleared through a clearing house. Under this new regime, sufficiently liquid and standardized over-the-counter derivatives transactions are required to be centrally cleared, and the most liquid of those are required to be executed on platforms. However, some derivatives, whose terms are privately negotiated between two parties, will remain uncleared. These non-centrally cleared swaps will be subject to new margin requirements based on an international standard developed by the Basel Committee on Banking Supervision and the International Organization of Securities Commissions.

Deliverable Interest Rate Swap futures

Deliverable interest rate swap forwards are a new product designed to sidestep some of the new regulations in the swap markets. They allow investors to trade interest rate swaps on a forward basis with the financial protections attendant to a standard futures contract. As such, they blend the advantages of trading both futures and over-the-counter derivative instruments in a consolidated package. The drawbacks to swap futures are that the end user has to post initial margin as well as "variation" margin and is exposed to basis risk.

Chapter 15 Questions

1. The Republic of Elbonia issues bonds in their own currency and in Euros. Which is likely to be considered more secure? Explain.

2. What is a repurchase agreement? Why might a repurchase agreement have low credit risk?

3. In the fixed-income world, what is meant by the term 'bootstrapping?'

4. Explain what credit spread means.

5. Suppose you are a fixed income trader at a large investment bank and you believe that interest rates are likely to rise more than the yield curve would suggest over the next year. Would you rather pay fixed or pay floating on a plain vanilla interest rate swap?

6. A one year risk-free zero-coupon bond pays 4%, a two year risk-free zero-coupon bond pays 6%. What does the market expect the one year risk-free zero-coupon bond to be paying in one year's time?

7. What is the purpose of a forward rate agreement?

8. Why do swaps always include one leg with uncertain cash flows?

9. Explain the role of the notional principal in a swap transaction. Why is the notional exchanged in a currency swap but not exchanged in a plain vanilla interest rate swap?

10. Why are floating interest rates different from fixed interest rates? If a fixed rate mortgage is available at an interest rate of 5% and a floating rate mortgage is available at 4% should you always borrow at the lower of the two rates?

11. Two companies have the following borrowing costs on a five year loan for $100million.

Company	Fixed Rate	Floating Rate
ABC	5.0%	LIBOR+0.1%
XYZ	6.5%	LIBOR+0.5%

If an intermediary is taking out 0.1% per year as a fee, design a swap that will be equally beneficial to both counterparties.

12. ABC wishes to borrow British pounds (GBP) at a fixed interest rate, XYZ wishes to borrow US dollars (USD) at a fixed interest rate. They both need to borrow the same amount of money in dollar terms. Their borrowing rates in each currency are shown in the table below.

Company	USD	GBP
ABC	5.0%	6.0%
XYZ	6.0%	6.3%

If an intermediary is taking out 0.50% per year as a fee, design a swap that will be equally beneficial to both counterparties.

13. What is the difference between a swap broker and a swap dealer?

14. Suppose that a swap has been in existence for some time already and that we now are looking to value it. Suppose that it pays floating 6 month LIBOR versus 6% fixed, semi-annually. It is on a $100 million notional and has 1.75 years remaining. Suppose we know that LIBOR continuously compounded is 3%,

3.5%, 3.7%, and 4.3% for the 3 month, 9 month, 15 month, and 21 month periods. We are also aware that the last 6-month LIBOR price was 3.2%. What is the value of this swap?

15. Is the expected loss from a default on a swap the same as the expected loss on the default of a loan with the same principal amount? Explain.

16. Value an interest rate swap where a bank is paying 7% annually and is receiving 3-month LIBOR in return on a notional principal of $100 million with payments exchanged quarterly. The swap has 14 months remaining. The swap rate for 3-month LIBOR is 8% for all maturities. The 3-month LIBOR rate one month ago was 7.4% per annum. Assume all rates are compounded quarterly.

Chapter 16

RISK MANAGEMENT AND FINANCIAL DERIVATIVES

Managing risk is central to managing any financial institution. Risk is the potential that a chosen action (or inaction) leads to an undesirable outcome. Potential losses may also be called "risks." Managing financial risk is as much about exploiting opportunities for gain as it is about avoiding losses. Successful financial firms are those that effectively manage all risks, controlling the downside and exploiting the upside.

Risk management involves identifying risks, prioritizing them, and utilizing resources in an economical manner to control the probability and impact of unfortunate events. This must be done while allowing the firm to take sensible risks that drive profitability.

Sources of Financial Risk

Within a financial institution there are numerous sources of risk. Table 16.1 is a list that is by no means complete of the various sources of risk within a financial institution.

Table 16.1 Sources of Risk	
Equity risk	Counterparty risk
Credit risk	Litigation risk
Foreign exchange risk	Reputation risk
Interest rate risk	Accidents
Inflation risk	Operational risk
Liquidity risk	Fraud risk
Volatility risk	Full cycle costs
Sector risk (diversification)	Terrorism
Environmental risk	Social/health risks
Computer hacking	

Risk Management Strategies

Once risks have been identified, a variety of strategies exist to manage them. The risk can be transferred to another party, for example by insuring against it. The risk can be avoided, for example by avoiding a risky activity or investment. Some of the negative effects of the risk can be reduced by hedging. The firm may choose to accept some or all of the consequences of a particular risk, because avoiding it may be too costly, the risk may be assessed as quite remote, or taking that risk may be core to the firm's strategy and profitability goals.

Principles of Risk Management

According to the International Organization for Standardization, risk management should:

- Create value
- Be an integral part of organizational processes
- Be part of decision making
- Explicitly address uncertainty
- Be systematic and structured
- Be based on the best available information
- Be tailored

- Take into account human factors
- Be transparent and inclusive
- Be dynamic, iterative, and responsive to change
- Be capable of continual improvement and enhancement

The Importance of Prioritization

The risks with the greatest loss and the greatest probability of occurring should be dealt with first, and risks with lower probability of occurrence and lower loss are handled next in probability order. The process of risk measurement and risk management can be difficult. Balancing among risks with a high probability of occurrence but lower loss, versus a risk with high loss but a lower probability of occurrence is always going to be a challenge.

What is Risk Retention?

No organization can fully avoid or mitigate all risk, simply because of financial and practical limitations. Therefore, all organizations have to accept some level of residual risk. The concept of self insurance falls into this category. If self insurance is approached as a serious risk management technique, money is set aside using actuarial information such that the amount set aside is sufficient to cover the future potential loss. Self insurance or risk retention is a reasonable strategy for small risks where the cost of insuring against the risk might be greater over time than the total losses likely to be sustained. All risks that are not avoided or transferred are retained by default; this includes risks that are so large that they either cannot be insured against or that the premiums would be unfeasible.

Business continuity planning is a group of processes and contingencies put in place to deal with the consequences of realized residual risks. A business continuity plan is a plan to continue business operations in the case of a disaster. Such a plan typically prepares for how a business would recover its operations, move operations to another location, or in the worst case scenario unwind its operations after damage by events like natural disasters, terrorist attacks, or outbreak of war. For example, if a flood destroys a data center, the data should be backed up at multiple sites and in multiple formats so that it can be quickly recovered and operations can continue as normal.

Risk Management on The Trading Floor

Risk management is a specialized field, and whole books have been written on topics that we have covered above in just a sentence or two. While there are many sources of financial risk, we will be concentrating here on *market risk* meaning the risk of unexpected changes in market prices. Our chapter on the Greeks gives a lot of useful information to traders who are managing a portfolio of options within a financial institution. Financial institutions will calculate all of the Greeks on a daily or more frequent basis. This risk information provides traders and desk heads useful information, but when combined with risk information for all of the different departments of a large financial institution, such calculations can become of limited use to senior management.

Value at risk (VaR) is an attempt to measure risk, and put it in the format of a single number so that financial risk can be quickly explained and understood.

VaR is defined as the predicted loss at a specific confidence level, usually 95% or 99%, over a certain period of time. The VaR risk measure defines risk as mark-to-market loss on a fixed portfolio over a fixed time horizon.

For example, if a portfolio of stocks has a one-day 95% VaR of $1 million, there is a 5% chance that the portfolio will fall in value by $1 million or more, over a one day period, assuming markets are normal and that no changes are made to the portfolio. Another way of thinking about this is that a loss of $1 million or more is expected in this portfolio one day in every 20-day period (see Figure 16.1).

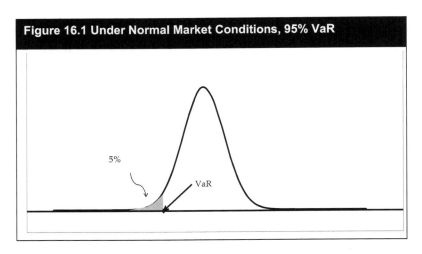

Figure 16.1 Under Normal Market Conditions, 95% VaR

The Emergence of VaR

VaR emerged in the late 1980s and early 1990s triggered by the 1987 crash. Many quantitative trading desks at large financial institutions claim to have been using the concept of VaR before 1990, but at that point it was not referred to as VaR and no large institutions had implemented it firm-wide. JP Morgan was the first bank to use VaR business-wide, to make sure different desks were not all exposed to the same risks. It was known as the 4:15 report, as the CEO Dennis Weatherstone demanded that a report combining all of the firms risk on one page be available to him within 15 minutes of the markets 4 p.m. close. JP Morgan published the methodology in 1994, and in 1996 spun off the methodology into RiskMetrics Group, where it could be implemented at other firms. In 1997, the SEC required public corporations to disclose quantitative information about their derivatives activity and VaR started turning up in financial statements. In 1999, the Basel II accord listed VaR as the preferred measure of market risk.

The Daily Convention

It is worth mentioning at this point that in our chapters on options and option pricing, volatility was usually spoken about in terms of "volatility per year." In VaR calculations, we are usually talking about daily losses, and for that reason we talk about "volatility per day." When the distribution is stable, one can translate VaR over different time periods.

$$VaR(T\,days) = VaR(1\,day)\sqrt{T}$$

Confidence Levels and VaR

VaR can be calculated at any confidence level. It is most common to talk about 95VaR and 99VaR. 95VaR can also be expressed as $VaR_{5\%}$ and 99VaR as $VaR_{1\%}$. It is usually referred to as a one day calculation or one day loss measure. In essence, these calculations answer the question, "what does a typical bad day look like?"

The Historical Approach vs. The Model Approach

There are two ways to calculate value at risk:

Historical: Look at the historical time series of a portfolio's returns and take the bottom q^{th} percentile. Microsoft Excel does this with the formula =percentile(array of returns,5%) to calculate 95VaR.

Model: Look at the expected standard deviation of the portfolio and use the normal distribution's tables to find the qth percentile.

Example: The Historical Approach

To quickly understand VaR, we will calculate it on the returns of an equity mutual fund (Vanguard's VFAIX). The last 15 years' daily percentage returns are plotted in Figure 16.2.

Daily returns are then ordered and converted into a histogram of daily returns (Figure 16.3).

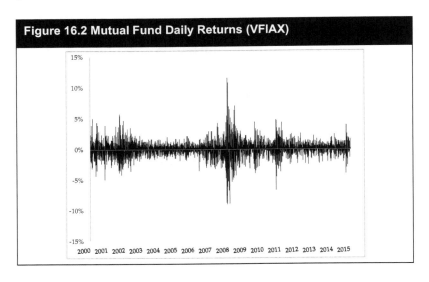

Figure 16.2 Mutual Fund Daily Returns (VFIAX)

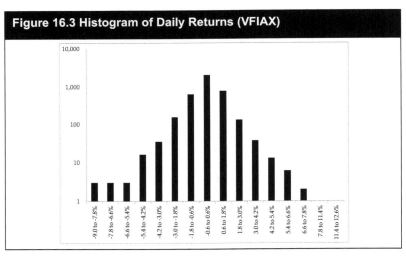

Figure 16.3 Histogram of Daily Returns (VFIAX)

In statistics, the "68–95–99 rule" is shorthand to remember the percentage of values around the mean in a normal distribution with a width of one, two, and three standard deviations. More accurately, 68.27%, 95.45%, and 99.73% of the values lie within one, two, and three standard deviations of the mean, respectively. VaR assumes normally distributed returns, implying 68% of the time we expect daily returns to fall between -1.23% and +1.29% (Figure 16.4).

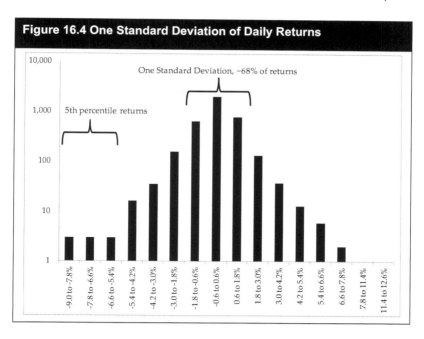

Figure 16.4 One Standard Deviation of Daily Returns

In the worst 5% of days, this portfolio will lose 6.6% or more, as shown in the left tail of Figure 16.4.

Example: The Model Approach

If a portfolio's standard deviation (σ) is expected to be 1.25% and we want to know its one-day 99% VaR, we use the normal distribution tables (see Figure 16.5). The closest to 1% is 0.99%, this is 2.33 standard deviations to the left of the mean. This means that the worst 1% of days, we expect to have a 2.33 standard deviation loss. We assume the expected daily return for the portfolio to be 0%. Hence, 2.33 × 1.25% standard deviation gives us 2.91%.

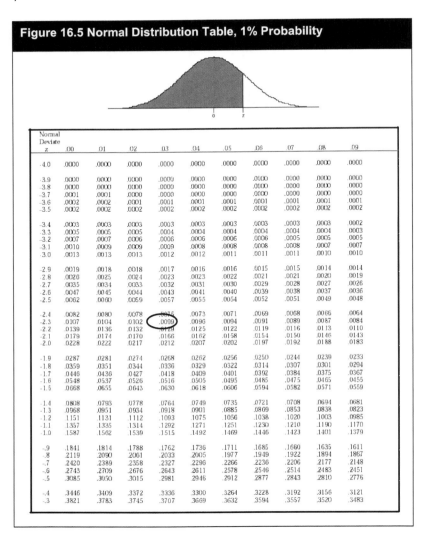

Figure 16.5 Normal Distribution Table, 1% Probability

Normal Deviate z	.00	.01	.02	.03	.04	.05	.06	.07	.08	.09
-4.0	.0000	.0000	.0000	.0000	.0000	.0000	.0000	.0000	.0000	.0000
-3.9	.0000	.0000	.0000	.0000	.0000	.0000	.0000	.0000	.0000	.0000
-3.8	.0000	.0000	.0000	.0000	.0000	.0000	.0000	.0000	.0000	.0000
-3.7	.0001	.0001	.0000	.0000	.0000	.0000	.0000	.0000	.0000	.0000
-3.6	.0002	.0002	.0001	.0001	.0001	.0001	.0001	.0001	.0001	.0001
-3.5	.0002	.0002	.0002	.0002	.0002	.0002	.0002	.0002	.0002	.0002
-3.4	.0003	.0003	.0003	.0003	.0003	.0003	.0003	.0003	.0003	.0002
-3.3	.0005	.0005	.0005	.0004	.0004	.0004	.0004	.0004	.0004	.0003
-3.2	.0007	.0007	.0006	.0006	.0006	.0006	.0006	.0005	.0005	.0005
-3.1	.0010	.0009	.0009	.0009	.0008	.0008	.0008	.0008	.0007	.0007
-3.0	.0013	.0013	.0013	.0012	.0012	.0011	.0011	.0011	.0010	.0010
-2.9	.0019	.0018	.0018	.0017	.0016	.0016	.0015	.0015	.0014	.0014
-2.8	.0026	.0025	.0024	.0023	.0023	.0022	.0021	.0021	.0020	.0019
-2.7	.0035	.0034	.0033	.0032	.0031	.0030	.0029	.0028	.0027	.0026
-2.6	.0047	.0045	.0044	.0043	.0041	.0040	.0039	.0038	.0037	.0036
-2.5	.0062	.0060	.0059	.0057	.0055	.0054	.0052	.0051	.0049	.0048
-2.4	.0082	.0080	.0078	.0075	.0073	.0071	.0069	.0068	.0066	.0064
-2.3	.0107	.0104	.0102	.0099	.0096	.0094	.0091	.0089	.0087	.0084
-2.2	.0139	.0136	.0132	.0129	.0125	.0122	.0119	.0116	.0113	.0110
-2.1	.0179	.0174	.0170	.0166	.0162	.0158	.0154	.0150	.0146	.0143
-2.0	.0228	.0222	.0217	.0212	.0207	.0202	.0197	.0192	.0188	.0183
-1.9	.0287	.0281	.0274	.0268	.0262	.0256	.0250	.0244	.0239	.0233
-1.8	.0359	.0351	.0344	.0336	.0329	.0322	.0314	.0307	.0301	.0294
-1.7	.0446	.0436	.0427	.0418	.0409	.0401	.0392	.0384	.0375	.0367
-1.6	.0548	.0537	.0526	.0516	.0505	.0495	.0485	.0475	.0465	.0455
-1.5	.0668	.0655	.0643	.0630	.0618	.0606	.0594	.0582	.0571	.0559
-1.4	.0808	.0793	.0778	.0764	.0749	.0735	.0721	.0708	.0694	.0681
-1.3	.0968	.0951	.0934	.0918	.0901	.0885	.0869	.0853	.0838	.0823
-1.2	.1151	.1131	.1112	.1093	.1075	.1056	.1038	.1020	.1003	.0985
-1.1	.1357	.1335	.1314	.1292	.1271	.1251	.1230	.1210	.1190	.1170
-1.0	.1587	.1562	.1539	.1515	.1492	.1469	.1446	.1423	.1401	.1379
-.9	.1841	.1814	.1788	.1762	.1736	.1711	.1685	.1660	.1635	.1611
-.8	.2119	.2090	.2061	.2033	.2005	.1977	.1949	.1922	.1894	.1867
-.7	.2420	.2389	.2358	.2327	.2296	.2266	.2236	.2206	.2177	.2148
-.6	.2743	.2709	.2676	.2643	.2611	.2578	.2546	.2514	.2483	.2451
-.5	.3085	.3050	.3015	.2981	.2946	.2912	.2877	.2843	.2810	.2776
-.4	.3446	.3409	.3372	.3336	.3300	.3264	.3228	.3192	.3156	.3121
-.3	.3821	.3783	.3745	.3707	.3669	.3632	.3594	.3557	.3520	.3483

The worst 1% of days should involve losses of 2.91% or greater. If we multiply this return by the size of the portfolio, we will get 99 VaR in dollar terms. For a $1 million portfolio, one would expect to lose $29,125 or more on the worst 1% of days in normal markets.

The Constant Volatility Assumption

In a standard VaR calculation, the volatility estimate is constant. The problem with this constant volatility method is that substantial evidence exists showing that volatility is not constant from day to day but rather varies over time and tends to cluster. Volatility clustering means that a period of increased (decreased) volatility is frequently followed by a period of high (low) volatility that persists for some time. Time-varying volatility with clustering seems to be a general feature of asset prices. Consequently, using the constant volatility method to calculate VAR could be very misleading.

When the expected return and volatility don't vary from day to day, the VaR estimate does not vary either. But if the volatility is changing from day to day, the VaR must also be changing.

If volatility changes every day, VaR becomes significantly more complicated. How do we know today's likely volatility? The most common solution to this problem was introduced in 1986 by Tim Bollerslev. Bollerslev's time-varying volatility technique, called the GARCH method (GARCH stands for generalized autoregressive conditional heteroskedasticity), allows us to base our prediction of today's volatility on recent volatility.

The daily volatility estimate using GARCH is a weighted average of past squared returns, just as it was in the constant volatility case. The difference is that the constant volatility method weights past squared returns equally while the GARCH method weights recent squared returns more heavily than distant returns.

The GARCH method works better for currencies than it does for stock prices as stock volatility goes up more as a result of a recent large negative return than it does as a result of a recent large positive return. GARCH volatility estimates don't depend on whether yesterday's return was positive or negative. Thus, this method can't allow for stock volatility's asymmetric response to past returns. Asymmetric volatility methods exist for stock prices that take this into account.

Once we have an estimate of today's expected volatility from the GARCH model, we can multiply the confidence factor times the square root of today's volatility times today's stock price to find today's VaR. When we use the GARCH method, the confidence factor is the only number that does not change daily.

Risk Management of Derivatives

Many portfolios contain derivatives such as futures, options, and swaps. In the case of a derivative on an equity, we know how to find the VaR of the equity over a one-day horizon at the 99 percent confidence level—we just find the volatility of its return and multiply its square root by the product of today's stock price and the confidence factor. But how can we find the VaR of a derivative on this stock?

One approach is to link the derivative to the underlying stock and use the standard VaR method. To do this, we use a pricing method, such as the Black-Scholes model, to calculate delta, which gives us a way to translate the derivative portfolio into the stock portfolio. Delta tells us how the derivative's price changes when the stock price changes a small amount. So, using our estimate of the stock's volatility, we could calculate VaR as we did before: by multiplying delta times the square root of the stock's volatility times the confidence factor.

An obvious drawback to this method is that it will work only when stock price changes are small. For larger changes, delta itself can change dramatically, leading to inaccurate VaR estimates. Thus, we need to account for how delta changes (gamma), complicating the analysis.

To deal with this complication, risk managers often use Monte Carlo analysis. Using the volatility and covariance estimates for the derivatives' underlying assets as well as a pricing tool, risk managers can then look at the largest loss the derivative will sustain for 99% of the likely outcomes. Let's suppose this loss is $100. Then the VaR of the derivative over a one-day horizon at the 99 percent confidence level is $100.

This Monte Carlo approach can be applied to other portfolios with short volatility payoffs such as merger arbitrage and event-driven strategies.

VaR: An Imperfect Model

There are several flaws in the Value at Risk calculation:

- VaR assumes normally distributed returns. Many assets have fat-tailed, left-skewed distributions. In these situations, VaR will greatly understate expected losses.
- VaR assumes that a portfolio is static, which is rarely the case.
- Just because 95VaR predicts that you will have losses of x% on twelve days of the year, that does not mean that these days will be evenly spaced. They could occur sequentially.
- VaR drastically underestimates correlations in a crisis. In market crises, when traders rush to exit positions and reduce portfolios, risk assets tend to become *more* correlated.

Common abuses in the Value at Risk calculation are:

1. Thinking of VaR as a worst-case loss.
2. Believing that losses will be less than some multiple, often three, of VaR.
3. Making VaR reduction the central concern of risk management.

VaR on the Trading Floor?

The entire point of VaR is to attempt to measure risk and put it in the format of a single number so that financial risk can be quickly explained and understood. This is particularly useful to managers of large complex financial institutions where they may not necessarily understand the specific risks being taken on various desks, but they would like to know if the overall risk level is increasing or decreasing. It is designed to give them a single number to look at, so they can then dig deeper to understand how concentrated risks might be, and where and why these risks are being taken in the various departments that they oversee. While this may make sense, VaR can be easy to misunderstand, and can be dangerous when misunderstood. For a senior manager, concentrating on this one number, which claims to estimate the risk of rare events, can give false confidence and can lead to excessive risk-taking and leverage at financial institutions.

If senior management is to judge risk exposure by one number, this can be exploited by traders. Traders within these institutions are usually quite aware of the risk metrics that they are being judged by and as such, VaR can create an incentive for them to take excessive but remote risks.

The use of VaR when you have just experienced a very benign volatility environment in the markets can be very misleading.

Losses are measured by assuming that the assets can be sold at current market prices. However, if a firm has highly illiquid assets, VaR may underestimate the true losses, since the assets may have to be sold at a discount.

In the two years following July 2007, markets experienced twenty days of ten or greater standard deviation moves. As a reference point, 6 sigma events should occur according to the normal distribution once every 1.5 million years, and 10 sigma events are considerably less likely to occur. Whenever a model predicts that something has almost no chance of failure, the probability that the model can fail becomes important. Quite often that probability overshadows the predicted risk by many orders of magnitude.

Conditional Value at Risk

Conditional Value at Risk is related to VaR, but is more conservative. Conditional Value at Risk calculates the average of the losses in the worst q% of cases. VaR might tell you that a loss of $1 million or greater is a VaR99% break. Conditional Value at Risk would calculate the average return of all of those worst 1% of days. This figure at a given confidence level will always be a larger negative number than VaR at that confidence level.

Stress Testing

In addition to calculating VaR, financial institutions will also carry out *stress testing*. Stress testing involves testing how a portfolio would have performed in extreme market conditions. For example, how would a portfolio perform if the stock market fell by 10% and implied volatility went up 300% in a day? How would a portfolio have held up during the 1987 crash, on September 11, 2001, or during the worst days of the financial crisis of 2007-2008. *Stressed VaR* (SVaR) is a measure of market risk tailored to stressed market conditions. This measure incorporates scenario analysis in a standard VaR setting.

Conclusion

Successful risk management is in the details. While there are a lot of useful formulas out there to help the risk manager, the subjective component of risk management is significant. A good risk manager at a financial institution spends a lot of time out on the trading floor talking to the traders trying to understand their way of thinking, what sort of risks they think are reasonable, and trying to understand the engine that generates the firm's profits. A risk manager who only looks at the risk numbers generated by a numerical risk system is never going to understand the true risks that the firm or portfolio is exposed to. Hedge fund manager David Einhorn compared VaR to "an airbag that works all the time, except when you have a car accident." While VaR has many flaws, it adds value as a tool of risk management. Like all of the formulas used in quantitative finance, VaR suffers from the "garbage in, garbage out" problem. In quantitative finance, we use many formulas that can seem very exciting to a beginner. These formulas are often derived from physics or engineering, and to those who don't know better they seem to give rock solid answers. The perfect price for this option is… or the risk on our books is… In finance, unlike in physics or engineering, most of the inputs are predictions, rough estimates, or numbers that for a variety of reasons can change very quickly. The formulas that we use help us to compare value, or give us a way of understanding the risk on the books today compared to the risk on the books last month. Financial mathematics is extremely useful to an investor or risk manager who always keeps in mind the assumptions that are underlying the various formulas, and is aware of how these things can break down. A student of finance and risk management should spend some time studying financial history. While every financial crisis is different, important lessons can be learned from the past.

Chapter 16 Questions

1. List eight sources of risk within a financial institution.

2. Once risks have been identified within an institution, what are the next steps in dealing with them?

3. Explain the concept of risk retention. Why might a financial institution choose to do this?

4. What is business continuity planning?

5. What is the difference between VaR and expected shortfall?

6. How are the Greeks used to manage risk?

7. If you were managing a $100,000 two-asset portfolio, with each asset equally weighted. If each asset has a daily volatility of 1% and their correlation coefficient is 0.8, what is the 5-day 95% VaR for the portfolio?

8. Explain why the standard VaR model might have difficulty estimating the risk characteristics of a portfolio of options.

9. What is the definition of 95% VaR?

10. Could a portfolio of assets ever lose more that 3× its 99% VaR?

11. Explain two advantages and two disadvantages of using VaR in risk management of a large financial institution like an investment bank.

12. A firm has a 95% VaR of 3%. How frequently should they expect to see losses of 3% or greater in their portfolio?

13. If a portfolio has a daily volatility of 1.25%, using the normal distribution table (Figure 16.6) what is the 95% VaR of the portfolio?

14. Explain what a GARCH model is and how it might be useful to a risk manager.

15. Why might asymmetric volatility methods be used for certain asset classes instead of GARCH?

16. Describe three common abuses of VaR.

17. How does stress testing work within a risk management framework?

Chapter 17

CREDIT & CREDIT DERIVATIVES

Credit is the trust that allows one party to obtain goods or resources from another party where that second party does not pay immediately, but instead arranges to either pay or return those resources at a later date. Credit encompasses any form of deferred payment. Examples include home mortgages, credit card debts, corporate borrowing, and government borrowing. The concept of credit is necessary whenever something is borrowed or lent.

Credit risk is the risk that a deferred payment agreement may be reneged on at or before the time schedule for reimbursement. This is the risk of default, and credit risk is also known as default risk or counterparty risk. In practice, the majority of the credit market takes place through the issuance of debt or loans.

Historically, debt obligations were entered into and the counterparties to the transaction did not change throughout the life of the loan, until the debt matured. Credit risk is most thoroughly examined at the initiation of the loan, and then monitored periodically until maturity. Loans and bonds can however be traded throughout their lives, between a variety of market participants. Thus, the concept of credit risk expands to bring in credit deterioration or credit improvement, and not just the binary outcomes of "borrower repays" or "borrower defaults." Considerable sums of money can be made and lost by traders through these more subtle variations in credit quality and pricing throughout the life of a bond. Credit risk is better defined as the risk of gains or losses arising from changes in credit quality.

Bond Credit Ratings

Credit rating agencies exist to provide investors an independent measure of the credit quality of issuing firms and individual debt instruments. The largest credit rating agencies are: S&P, Moody's, and Fitch. These companies are paid a fee by the debt-issuing entity to provide an independent credit rating which is then shared widely with public debt market participants.

Figure 17.1 shows the different credit grades issued by the big three ratings agencies to classify the risks of credit instruments.

Rated bonds are broken down into two large categories, investment-grade and speculative-grade (also known as "junk bonds"). Unrated bonds are also considered to be speculative grade. The threshold between investment-grade and speculative-grade ratings has important market implications for issuers' borrowing costs. Many institutional investors have policies that require them to limit their bond investments to investment-grade issues. Some classes of investor are legally required to only invest in investment-grade bonds and must sell a bond holding if it gets downgraded to speculative grade.

Figure 17.1 Credit Rating Agency Rankings

Moodys	S & P	Fitch		Definition
Aaa	AAA	AAA		Prime, maximum safety
Aa1	AA+	AA+		Very high grade/quality
Aa2	AA	AA		Very high grade/quality
Aa1	AA-	AA-	Investment Grade	Very high grade/quality
A1	A+	A+		Upper medium quality
A2	A	A		Upper medium quality
A3	A-	A-		Upper medium quality
Baa1	BBB+	BBB+		Lower medium grade
Baa2	BBB	BBB		Lower medium grade
Baa3	BBB-	BBB-		Lower medium grade
Ba1	BB+	BB+		Speculative
Ba2	BB	BB		Speculative
Ba3	BB-	BB-		Speculative
B1	B+	B+		Highly speculative
B2	B	B	Speculative Grade	Highly speculative
B3	B-	B-		Highly speculative
Caa1	CCC+	CCC+		Substantial risk
Caa2	CCC	CCC		In poor standing
Caa3	CCC-	CCC-		In poor standing
Ca	CC	CC		Extremely speculative
C	C+,C,C-	C+,C,C-		Maybe in or extremely close to default
	D	D		Default

The risks associated with investment-grade bonds are considered to be significantly higher than those of government bonds. The difference between rates for first-class government bonds and investment-grade bonds is called the investment-grade spread. Some view the range of this spread as an indicator of the stability of the economy. Higher investment-grade spreads imply a weaker economy.

Credit ratings can have a tremendous impact on the price of financial instruments. Prior to the existence of ratings agencies, investors had difficulty obtaining and processing sufficient information about creditworthiness to make informed credit risk decisions. Unlike the equities market, where typically a company would have only one equity security outstanding in public markets, a company could have a wide range of debt instruments outstanding, each with different maturities, different coupons, varying legal covenants, ranges of collateralization, and seniority of repayment in the event of default. The fact that each issue was rated separately reduced the confusion surrounding these instruments and greatly increased the attractiveness to investors of investing in bonds, including small investors who previously would have found this research effort prohibitive. Ratings information greatly enhanced liquidity in bond markets.

The History of Credit Derivatives

In the past, banks made loans and mortgages to companies and individuals and typically held that risk until maturity of the loans, funded by their own client deposits. This introduced a series of limitations on the loan and mortgage markets.

A given bank might aim to have a diversified set of outstanding loans to companies. Loaning to a portfolio of companies across industry sectors, and applying strict percentage caps on loans to individual sectors should minimize losses in the event of a significant downturn in one industry sector. The bank might mandate a maximum 10% of its loan portfolio to mining companies and insist that these amounts be spread across a number of different companies to reduce the default risk of exposure to one company. These sector loan restrictions, designed to make the bank's portfolio safer from defaults, reduced loan capacity to individual companies.

The former hold-to-maturity loan model constrained the bank's portfolio composition. The bank would only be able to make limited numbers and sizes of loans to companies that they otherwise might be very confident of lending more funds to. Companies received fewer loans under this model due to the banks' constraints.

A further drawback was the fact that a bank might have an industry or regional expertise that it could profitably and successfully pursue but would be restrained by industry sector weight constraints in the portfolio. The bank might have a top-tier mining industry team, one that measures mining credit risk with acute precision and has extensive local relationships with the mining community. This proficiency could not be used to its full capacity in the hold-to-maturity loan environment. At the same time, there were other investors in the broader financial world who were interested in taking on these credit risk exposures.

A similar effect was seen in bank lending for home mortgages, credit cards and student loans markets.

This mismatch of banks' ability to underwrite a far greater number of loans than they could feasibly hold, combined with a broader investor appetite to hold credit risk helped to drive the credit derivatives market.

What are Credit Derivatives?

Credit derivatives are financial instruments that have payoffs that depend on corporate or sovereign bonds, or on loan portfolios as the underlying instruments. They transfer the credit risk from one party to another without transferring ownership of the underlying securities. The underlying securities need not be owned by *either* party in the transaction. The most common types of credit derivatives are *asset backed securities*, *credit default swaps*, and *collateralized debt obligations*.

Securitization was developed to ameliorate the problem of banks' ability to issue larger amounts of credit than they could hold to maturity on their own balance sheets. Securitization is the process of creating securities whose value and income payments are derived from and collateralized by a specified pool of underlying assets.

Financial Securitization

Securitization brought about numerous changes in debt markets. It allowed originators to remove loan assets from their balance sheets, which increased overall lending much faster than deposit growth alone would have. Banks competed for loan, mortgage, credit card, and bond origination business, leading to decreased borrowing costs for companies and individuals. The increased availability of loans brings down borrowing costs and allows people who historically were unable to borrow to have access to credit. The increased availability of credit affects demand for and thus the price of real estate and other assets that can be purchased on credit.

When a bank made a loan and kept that loan on its books, the credit risk of the loan mattered to the long-term profitability and survival of the bank. Securitization allows financial institutions to make loans that they do not intend to keep on their books. When loans are made in this manner, there is less of an incentive to accurately measure and monitor credit risk. Originators are instead incentivized to minimize the costs associated with qualifying the borrower and monitoring their credit risk. This can lead to a decrease in overall credit quality.

What are Asset Backed Securities?

Asset backed securities (ABS), are bonds or notes backed by financial assets. The asset pool is usually a group of small and illiquid assets that would be difficult to sell individually. Pooling these assets into financial instruments allows them to be sold to investors such as other banks, hedge funds, insurance companies, and pension funds.

The pool of potential underlying assets is extensive. It can include individuals' credit card receivables, mortgage loans, student loans, auto loans, trade receivables, aircraft and other equipment leases, royalty payments, and movie revenues.

When creating an ABS, the originating bank usually sets up a separate institution, called a *special purpose vehicle* (SPV), to handle the securitization. This is a separate company that creates and sells the asset backed securities and uses the proceeds to pay back the bank that originated the underlying assets. This is to keep the asset backed securities at arms-length from the issuing bank, such that if there are failures of the securities over time, they remain separate from the performance and credit results of the bank that initially created them.

The pools of assets are packaged into a tradable instrument whose value depends on the performance and cash flows of the underlying pool of individual assets. Once the assets have been packaged and transferred to the SPV, the originating bank can remove the assets from its own balance sheet, receiving cash in return. The asset backed securities are sold on to other financial institutions or investors. This transaction often improves the credit rating of the originating bank as well as reduces the amount of regulatory capital it is required to hold against its other business activities.

The asset backed securities are usually rated by credit rating agencies, and are evaluated based only on the assets and liabilities of the SPV. This rating can be higher than the credit rating of the issuing bank as the risks of the asset backed securities are no longer associated with the other risks that the originating bank might bear. This ring-fencing can improve the credit rating of the originating institution, reducing the interest rate that it has to pay on its debt obligations.

What are Credit Card Receivables?

Securities backed by credit card receivables have been a key part of the ABS market since they were first introduced in 1987. Credit card holders may borrow funds on a revolving basis up to an assigned credit limit. The borrowers then pay principal and interest as desired, along with the required minimum monthly payments.

Because principal repayment is not scheduled, credit card debt does not have an actual maturity date and is considered a non-amortizing loan. The fact that credit card receivable securities are non-amortizing and uncollateralized are the key differentiators from other fixed income securities.

What are CDO's

Collateralized debt obligations or CDOs are a type of asset backed security where the underlying assets are bonds or other financial assets. A portfolio of bonds is assembled and the risks of losses on the entire portfolio are carved up and sold to different investor classes. The first CDO was issued in 1987 by Drexel Burnham Lambert Inc.

CDOs can be thought of as a pool of bonds that promises to deliver cash flows to investors in a prescribed sequence. This sequence is based on the cash flow the CDO collects from the pool of bonds or other assets that it owns.

A CDO is made up of "tranches" or slices, which deliver the cash flow from interest and principal payments from the pool of bonds in sequence based upon seniority. If some bonds default and the cash collected by the CDO is not sufficient to pay all of its investors, those in the lowest, most "junior" tranches are allocated losses first. The last tranche to suffer losses from defaults are the safest, most senior tranches of the CDO. As a consequence of these different treatments, credit ratings and interest rates vary by tranche with the safest/most senior tranches paying the lowest rates and the riskiest tranches paying the highest rates to compensate these investors for the higher default risk. A CDO might be made up of the following tranches in order of security (see Figure 17.2): Senior AAA (or "super senior"); Junior AAA; AA; A; BBB; and Residual. The residual tranche is sometimes referred to as the "equity tranche" and is often retained by the issuer of the CDO, as it can be very difficult to find a buyer for it.

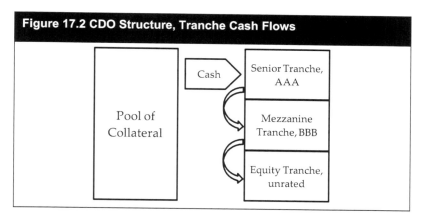

Figure 17.2 CDO Structure, Tranche Cash Flows

Early CDOs were diversified, and were made up of a mix of loans and debt securities from a variety of industries and of a variety of types including mortgages, student loans, aircraft leases, and credit card debt. This diversification was a selling point, as it implied that if there was a downturn in one sector and their loans defaulted, other types of debt would be less affected. The biggest selling point of CDOs was that they offered returns that were sometimes 2-3 percentage points higher than similarly rated corporate bonds. CDO issuance grew from $69 billion in 2000 to around $500 billion in 2006, much of this growth was due to the demand for yield in a low interest rate environment.

In practice, the pooling of a series of low-quality (lower grade or more speculative credit risk) assets can result in the creation of some higher-ranked credit products due to the tranching of the derivatives. CDOs are usually structured such that the highest tranche would receive a AAA (highest credit quality) rating. By 2003, as the CDO market grew rapidly, subprime mortgages began to replace diversified portfolios of loans as collateral. The global search for yield caused many investors to purchase CDOs, trusting the credit rating, without fully understanding the risks. By 2004, *mortgage-backed securities* (MBS) accounted for more than half of the collateral in CDOs and the demand for new CDOs began to drive the market for mortgage origination, in particular for lower credit quality loans. Toward the peak of the credit boom, there was so much more demand for CDOs than supply of loans that CDOs were being created by packaging up the low rated tranches of MBS and CDOs. "Synthetic CDOs" became a popular product in the mid-2000s where the underlying was a pool of CDS (a type of credit derivative described later in this chapter) not actual bonds. CDO-Squared was a term used to describe collateralized debt obligations backed primarily by the lower rated tranches of other CDOs.

The Importance of Default Correlation

A pool of loans might be expected to experience a certain level of individual borrower defaults, but they should, under normal circumstances, not all happen at the same time. During times of financial crisis, defaults become more highly correlated. This is particularly the case for the most stressed borrowers, whose loans increasingly made up the pools underlying CDOs.

The default correlation assumed in pricing CDOs is key. If the correlation is low, the senior tranches are very safe and the junior tranche is extremely risky. As the correlation gets higher, the junior tranches become less risky (relatively), and the senior tranches become more risky. If the correlation is 1, then the junior and senior tranches are equally risky.

Leading up to the financial crisis of 2007-2008, masses of CDOs and other, similar instruments were created. CDOs embed within their pricing, and in particular embed within their ratings, various default assumptions. These were calculated by large numbers of credit and mortgage performance experts using complex models. The models were often built and run by physicists and, in the end, the real-world correlations and default probabilities varied significantly from the models designed by banks, insurance companies, and asset managers.

CDOs and the Financial Crisis of 2007-2008

CDO issuance fell dramatically after the financial crisis of 2007-2008 (Figure 17.3) because so many investors experienced large losses in these products. CDOs, like everything else, suffer from the "garbage in, garbage out" problem. In essence, you cannot assemble a filet steak from low quality hamburger meat; however, there is value in the concept of taking a pool of assets and allocating the different risks and returns to investors with different risk profiles.

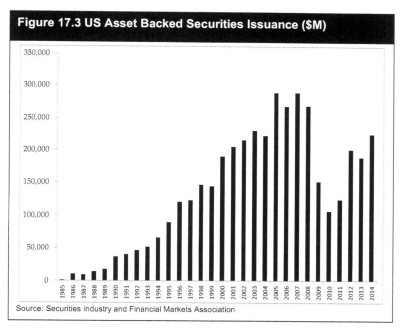

Figure 17.3 US Asset Backed Securities Issuance ($M)

Source: Securities Industry and Financial Markets Association

In 2013, the press reported on Deutsche Bank launching an $8.7 billion CDO with two tranches with interest rates ranging from 8% to 14.6%. In the low interest rate environment of 2013, investors in these products might at least be getting paid an interest rate that could compensate them for the risk they were taking. CDOs most likely won't go away, since in principle they have powerful risk management capabilities. Products like these allow for risk diversification that otherwise might be quite concentrated. Both banks and credit ratings agencies share significant responsibility for the CDO growth explosion, often when the issuers and ratings agencies knew the assets to be of poor underlying quality, in the mid 2000s, along with investors who were investing in products that they did not understand in the hopes of getting a "free lunch."

What are Credit Default Swaps?

Credit Default Swaps (CDS) are legal contracts that provide insurance against the risk of default by a company or country on its bonds. It is a swap agreement that the seller of the CDS will compensate the buyer in the event of a loan default or other credit event. The CDS buyer makes a series of payments (the CDS "fee" or "spread") to the seller and, in exchange, receives a payoff if the loan defaults (see Figure 17.4). CDS are the most widely traded credit derivatives.

Swaps sellers promise swap buyers a big payment if an entity's bonds or loans default. In return they receive quarterly payments. Neither needs to hold the underlying debt when entering into a CDS transaction. CDS are similar to other swaps in that they are valued at zero at inception, and later may incur gains or losses, depending on changes in the credit markets.

A company or country can be the underlying entity on which the contract/derivative is based, and these are called the *reference entity* in theW CDS market. A default by the reference entity is called a *credit event*.

The buyer of the insurance has the right to sell the bonds issued by the reference entity for full face value when a credit event occurs. The CDS insurance seller has the obligation to buy the bonds for full face value when a credit event occurs. The total face value is the swap's *notional value*. The buyer makes periodic payments to the seller until the maturity of the CDS contract or until a credit event occurs, typically quarterly or half-yearly. Settlement can involve physical delivery of the bonds or a cash settlement.

A CDS contract typically references the credit derivatives definitions as published by the International Swaps and Derivatives Association (ISDA). The confirmation typically specifies a reference entity that generally, although not always, has debt outstanding; and a reference obligation, usually an unsubordinated corporate bond or government bond. The life of the contract is specified by the effective date and termination date.

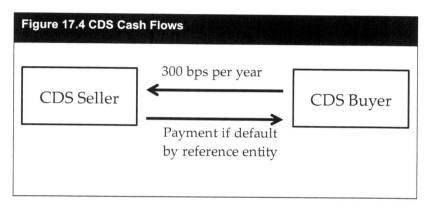

Figure 17.4 CDS Cash Flows

A CDS contract usually specifies that a number of different bonds issued by the reference entity can be delivered in the case of default. Usually these bonds will be of similar seniority, but they may trade at different prices after default. Should this occur, the buyer of CDS protection will search for the cheapest-to-deliver bond which they deliver to the CDS Seller in exchange for the insurance-like payout from the CDS contract in the event of reference entity default.

Many large financial institutions "make markets" in CDS on companies that they may never have lent any money to in the past. CDS market makers will then stand ready to buy or sell protection (and earn a spread between the two prices). Market makers can hedge their exposures by trading in the underlying bonds if needed. Most CDS contracts are five years in duration (but can be traded in other maturities).

Banks are large buyers of credit protection to hedge their loan books and insurance companies are the biggest sellers of CDS.

There are several events that can constitute a credit event and necessitate a payout on a CDS contract including bankruptcy, failure to pay (coupons or principal payments), or restructurings. The legal documents supporting the CDS contracts are very lengthy and potential investors would be wise to read carefully the definitions of specifically which corporate actions or events will be classified as credit events and legally entitle them to payouts.

The CDS spread refers to the price paid annually for protection on the bonds. This can also be compared to the spread over a risk-free rate at which the underlying reference entity's bonds trade. These should be very close, otherwise there would be arbitrage opportunities.

Typically, when a company goes bankrupt, there is some recovery for the bondholders from liquidation of the firm's assets. Usually expressed as a percentage of face value, and typically estimated to be 30%-40% of the face value of the bonds (based on historical bankruptcy payouts, each case is unique). CDS buyers receive the notional minus the recovery in a credit event.

CDS can be used to hedge a regular portfolio's bond holdings. Investors who are long bonds can buy CDS protection. So if the bond was paying out 6% per year, if the CDS costs 100 basis points (1% per year), they are left with a riskless bond position (effectively a government bond return rate) yielding 5% per year.

For example, if a CDS spread or cost of protection is trading at 300 basis points (bps), while the equivalent bond maturity yields 8%, and suppose the risk-free rate is 4%. The CDS is trading "too cheap," and investors could buy the bond, buy the CDS protection, and earn an arbitrage profit of 1% per year with no risk.

Credit market participants have created indices to track credit default swap spread movements. This can be a good real-time metric of risk in the bond markets. The most followed CDS index for US credit quality is the CDX, in Europe it's the ITRAXX.

A key feature of CDS valuation are the probabilities of default implied in their pricing. These can be backed out of market prices of the CDS and are called "implied probabilities of default."

The CDS market has been rapidly growing since the 1990s, and CDS are important tools for managing risks. However, they have come under significant regulatory scrutiny since banks and insurers held excessively large CDS positions that went sour in the financial crisis of 2007-2008.

Counterparty Risks

A CDS insurance buyer might be paying just 1-2% per year on a $10 million notional (approximately the smallest that anyone would trade), equating to just $100,000 to $200,000, but standing to gain $10 million in a credit event. If you pay this for half a year and then the reference entity defaults, you receive an extremely skewed payoff profile. Therefore, buyers worry considerably about counterparty risk in the CDS market.

Regulatory pressure has increased on trading CDS in a more transparent manner. The goal is to shift them from opaque OTC transactions onto exchanges and clearing houses, and to reduce counterparty risk.

Many traders in the CDS market do not favor an electronically-listed and cleared CDS market, since the increased transparency is usually accompanied by reduced bid-ask spreads for their market making activities.

In 2009, the Dodd-Frank Wall Street Reform and Consumer Protection Act mandated that swaps be regulated by the Commodity Futures Trading Commission (CFTC). It specifically required a clearing house be set up to trade and fairly price swaps. In the United States, ICE Clear Credit and the CME Group are two central counterparties for CDS.

Contrary to swaps tied to indexes, regulators haven't yet pushed most single-name credit swaps through central clearing houses. Instead they've largely remained bilateral transactions between dealers and clients, requiring higher capital charges under banking regulations. This has led investment banks to withdraw from the market and made trading credit default swaps more expensive.

How CDS Changed Credit Markets

Some market participants argue that CDS allowed lenders to issue loans without adequately assessing credit quality since lenders can sell all of the risks onto other investors and avoid credit evaluation and monitoring costs. The reduction in credit assessment should reduce borrowing costs as traditionally those evaluation and monitoring costs were passed through to borrowers in the form of higher interest rates.

Repackaging and distributing risk is superior in many ways in that more investors have access to the returns of a variety of credit issuers than they previously would; and risks are spread out to more investors, rather than concentrated within one financial institution. However, risk assessment might best be done by a lender in advance of a loan being made. The lender is in a unique position of access to bond issuers' senior management and can request documentation that small investors would struggle to attain. In a world with credit hedging, fewer difficult questions are asked of borrowers.

Problems With CDS

Critics of the CDS market have claimed that it has been allowed to become too large without proper regulation and that the CDS market has no transparency. Furthermore, there have been claims that CDS exacerbated the 2008 global financial crisis by hastening the demise of companies such as Lehman Brothers and AIG.

Financial commentators have argued that insurance markets where neither party has an insurable interest can lead to suboptimal social behavior. There have been cases where bondholders, who also own large amounts of CDS might aim to push for the company to enter bankruptcy in order to benefit from the credit event with their CDS. Many argue that purchasing insurance when you lack an insurable interest should be regulated and potentially made illegal.

CDS can give investors a false sense of security. For example, in 2012, the Greek government required bondholders to take a 75% loss on their holdings—CDS were not deemed to have experienced a "credit event" because the write down was mandated by Greek law. The realization that CDS provided no protection could have destroyed the CDS market, because borrowers like Greece could intentionally circumvent the CDS payout. However, after some delay, the ISDA ruled that these CDS should be considered to have experienced a credit event, and the buyers of protection on Greek debt had to be paid.

CDS are usually traded as a five year contract, and there is very little liquidity in "off the run" CDS. Traders might buy a CDS contract, and after a few weeks or months wish to sell it. They might do this by entering into a new, offsetting five year contract, which mostly hedges their exposure, but will leave some non-overlapping risk when the first contract rolls off and the other still has some time left. Regulations passed since the G-20 2009 Pittsburgh Agreement require portfolio compression from certain market participants which can be achieved through simultaneous novation[10],

---

[10] Novation refers to replacing one contractual obligation with another, or reassigning one counterparty name on a contract to another counterparty, and extinguishing the rights and liabilities of the original counterparty. Where numerous transactions between CDS counterparties could be simplified down to a significantly smaller number of counterparties due to cross-netting, novation can simplify the outstanding obligations down to the minimal number of counterparties to attain the same ultimate risk exposures. Novation of derivatives also refers to converting transactions originally struck between two private counterparties into transactions that now both face a clearing house,

cancellation, and/or amendment of multiple contracts, this is often facilitated through settlement of a cash-out sum.

Pricing Credit Default Swaps

There are two main approaches to pricing CDS contracts, the *probability model* and the *no-arbitrage approach*.

The Probability Model of Pricing CDS

The probability model takes the present value of the expected cash flows weighted by the probability of non-default.

The inputs to this model are: the premiums paid, the expected recovery rate in the event of a default, the credit curve of the reference entity, and the LIBOR curve in the market. For simplicity, the initial modeling is done assuming that a default, should it occur, happens only on premium payment dates (in practice, if a default occurs between payment dates, the buyer will owe a prorated premium to the CDS seller). A tree can be drawn of all of the possible outcomes or paths of the investment, where at each premium node, the reference entity defaults or not, and probabilities are assigned at each juncture to the events. A present value is taken of the probability-weighted cash flow outcomes. The probabilities of non-default at each juncture are calculated based on the credit spread curve of the underlying reference entity.

The No-Arbitrage Approach to Pricing CDS

The no-arbitrage model assumes that there is no risk-free arbitrage (and assumes no counterparty risk of the protection seller). Under this model, a CDS's price can be backed out of bond and swap

---

significantly reducing the counterparty risk faced by the two original counterparties.

spreads (over a risk-free benchmark such as LIBOR or US Treasuries). Suppose that a bond has a spread of 200bps over LIBOR and that the swap spread, the spread paid by the fixed-rate payer over the risk-free rate, is 60bps. This means that the CDS contract should trade at 140bps, otherwise an arbitrage would exist. However, there are sometimes reasons that, in practice, this tight pricing relationship does not hold, and in these situations the difference between the no-arbitrage price and the live trading price is called the "basis."

Credit Derivatives and the Financial Crisis of 2007 -2008

Easy availability of credit in the United States, fueled by low interest rates and reduced credit monitoring by financial institutions, led to a housing boom which facilitated debt-financed consumer spending. The existence of credit derivatives and securitization allowed financial institutions to make larger volumes of riskier loans than had been made in the past and consumers assumed an unprecedented debt load.

Between 1998 and 2006, the price of the typical American house increased by 124%. Between 1981 and 2001, the national median home price ranged from 2.9 to 3.1 times median household income. This rose to 4.6 times median household income in 2006.

When home prices declined in the latter half of 2007 and the secondary mortgage market collapsed, a global financial crisis was triggered. Credit derivatives were blamed by many for bringing about this crisis, or for intensifying it.

Credit ratings agencies are widely believed to have failed the markets in their calculations of credit risks on credit derivative products in the lead up to the financial crisis of 2007-2008. They relied on models that were given to them by the credit derivative issuers. The fact that they are paid by the security issuer, rather than the buyer, brought their impartiality into question. There is a structural conflict in this market whereby investors are the beneficiaries or ultimate end users of credit ratings calculations, yet the party paying for the ratings themselves is the issuer.

On the back of the financial crisis, politicians and regulators globally are pressuring originators to resume the former practice of maintaining at least some of the credit risks on the instruments they originate on their own balance sheets. Politicians face a trade-off of hoping to incentivize high consumer spending and home-ownership rates to boost GDP and achieve social goals associated with home-ownership while seeking to avoid the negative outcomes from widespread over-indebtedness from lax credit standards and real estate bubbles. Stronger credit controls stabilize an economy but reduce home values, decrease homeownership levels, and reduce an economy's GDP growth.

Chapter 17 Questions

1. What is credit?

2. What is the purpose of a credit ratings agency?

3. What is the difference between investment-grade bonds and speculative-grade bonds? Why might an investor choose to invest in either?

4. Are unrated bonds considered investment grade or speculative grade?

5. What are the advantages and disadvantages of securitization?

6. In terms of asset backed securities, what is a special purpose vehicle?

7. Explain how credit card receivables are a non-amortizing loan.

8. What is the purpose of a CDO?

9. Explain the structure of a CDO.

10. Explain how the CDO market collapsed during the financial crisis of 2007-2008.

11. Explain the importance of default correlation in pricing CDOs.

12. What is the risk difference between the two tranches of a two-tranche CDO if the assets in the pool are perfectly correlated to each other? Explain.

13. What is a CDS? How are the payments structured?

14. Can CDS be traded on a technology company that is entirely equity financed?

15. With regard to CDS, explain the terms "reference entity" and "notional value."

16. What is ISDA's role in the CDS market?

17. Explain some of the criticisms people might have about CDS.

18. What is a CDS index?

19. Explain the advantages and disadvantages associated with exchange-listed and cleared CDS contracts.

20. Describe the two approaches to pricing CDS.

21. A five year CDS on XYZ Industries requires semiannual payments of 75 basis points per year. The notional principal is $500 million. XYZ Industries defaults after four and a half years, a day after the semiannual payment is due. Three XYZ corporate bonds are available in the marketplace: Bond A is trading at 40% of its face value, Bond B is trading at 38% of its face value, and Bond C is trading at 41% of its face value. List the cash flows and their timing for the buyer of the CDS.

22. Explain what a synthetic CDO is and what a CDO squared is.

23. How might you expect the returns on the tranches of a CDO to change as the correlation of the assets in the underlying pool changes?

24. Explain what constitutes a credit event for a CDS contract.

25. What is the CDS seller economically doing, are they essentially buying bond exposure or are they selling bond exposure?

26. CDS need not be exclusively traded for expectations of default. CDS are also used to trade investors' differing viewpoints on the deterioration or improvement of an entity's credit quality. Explain how this might work.

Chapter 18

STRUCTURED FINANCIAL PRODUCTS

A *structured product*, also called a structured note, is an investment product usually made up of a bond and one or more derivatives. The purpose of structured products is to provide an investment payoff that is attractive to investors, and is differentiated from returns available in simple equity or fixed income markets. By combining a bond with, for example, a call option, investors can receive bond-like minimum returns, with potential for upside payoffs not available from a standard bond. Structured products are, in theory, any OTC investment product requiring tailoring or structuring to provide a specific risk exposure to suit customers' needs. The possibilities for what meets this criteria is enormous.

Structured products provide a means for investment banks to issue debt for themselves or other companies at lower than market interest rates. Prior to the creation of structured products, one of the only means to issuing sub-market coupon bonds was by issuing *convertible bonds* (which are in fact also a hybrid security, part-bond and part-option-like security). Adding option-like features to simple bonds enables banks to give investors something in exchange for a lower interest rate on debt. Structured products are generally difficult for unsophisticated investors to value, but offer unique and sometimes quite attractive payoff profiles, and thus

Investment banks added high mark-ups to the products, and they quickly became quite profitable for the issuers.

In practice, this usually involves a combination of a straight bond and an option of some sort. Figure 18.1 shows a common example of the basic components of a structured product.

Often structured products offer *principal guarantees* to the end investors. This means that an investor who invests $1000 on day one is "guaranteed" by the issuer to receive their $1000 back at maturity. Since there are no free lunches in economics, this means that the investor is giving up the interest on their money in the cases where they receive only their initial investment back.

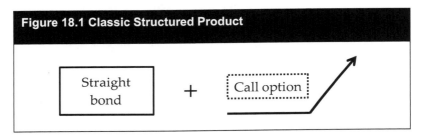

Figure 18.1 Classic Structured Product

In a principal-guaranteed structured product, with a five year duration, an investor invests $1000 at inception. The issuing counterparty, usually an investment bank, puts that money in a zero-coupon bond with a $1000 payoff at the end of year five. Zero-coupon bonds paying off $1000 in 5 years trade at a discount to par, and the cash differential is the amount that the issuing bank can take a portion of for its own fees and the remainder to purchase options that will provide some conditional promised return to the investor. In the event of the options expiring worthless, the investor receives only their initial $1000 back, financed by the zero-coupon bond. In the event of the options expiring in the money, the investor receives their $1000 initial investment back plus the option's payoff, minus the fees to the investment bank at the end of year five. Figure 18.2 illustrates the principal-guarantee payoff composition.

What are structurers offering investors in exchange for this loss of risk-free interest or credit-based interest on their initial capital investment? Investors put their money in structured products because they like the assurance that they will not have any losses in nominal terms, but under certain economic scenarios the opportunity to provide significantly better returns.

Many kinds of products or risk exposures can be put into the investment package of a structured product or principal guaranteed product. Many structured products have principal-guarantees or principal protection, however not all of them do. A principal guaranteed five year note with an initial investment of $1000 guarantees a minimum return at the end of year 5 of $1000. This is designed to make an investor feel that in the worst-case scenario no losses are incurred. However, due to the foregone risk-free interest over a five year period, the purchasing power of $1000 will have been eroded by inflation, and an investor would have been better off having invested at the risk free rate. The other key risk of principal guaranteed products is counterparty risk -- in particular the counterparty that is making the guarantee. In the vast majority of cases, principal guaranteed products are not government-backed guarantees, instead they are Investment bank backed guarantees (which comes with all of the credit risk relating to those issuers).

The options exposures underlying structured products are as varied as the structurers' imaginations.

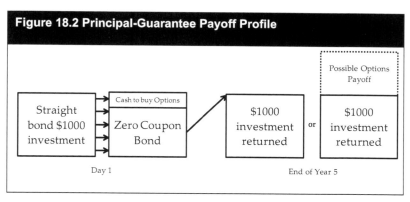

Figure 18.2 Principal-Guarantee Payoff Profile

Some of the most popular structured products give investors

exposures to the performance of: equity, commodities, foreign exchange, interest rates, inflation, and hedging of corporate risks.

Structured products first appeared in the United States but never gained wide reception in North America, largely due to consumer protections that require an investor to read and sign an options disclosure document in order to trade or invest in derivatives products. In the US, the OCC (Options Clearing Corporation) issues a 183 page form entitled, "Characteristics & Risks of Standardized Options" which is known as the ODD (Options Disclosure Document), first published in 1994. A requirement to sign off on having read and understood the ODD reduces the number of options participants significantly. This much stronger retail customer protection significantly reduced the proliferation of these products in North America. Structured products are widely available in Europe, where 96% of retail structured products are sold, with some of the largest investor bases in Spain and Italy (see Figure 18.3). They are often sold in retail banks as an alternative to savings accounts. Pending European Union rules will soon require banks to inform retail clients what could go wrong with these products. The EU Parliament and Council proposed mandatory disclosure to retail investors before they purchase structured products outlining information on the features, far more clearly stating the bank's structuring fees incurred by customers, and detailing the risks of structured products. These enhanced disclosures should help consumers to more easily understand and compare products.

Portfolio Insurance

The first examples of principal-protected structured products were known as *Constant Proportion Portfolio Insurance* (CPPI), and these involved investments with stop loss strategies in place to preserve principal. Instead of buying a zero-coupon bond and some options exposure, a portion of the investor's funds were placed in a risky asset, which would be liquidated if the prices fell through a targeted tolerance level, at which point the money could be invested in a bond where it would grow back to the initially invested amount of money over the life of the product.

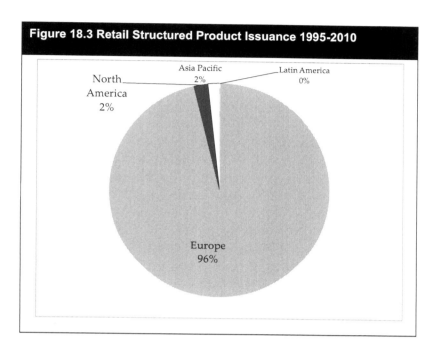

Figure 18.3 Retail Structured Product Issuance 1995-2010

CPPI caps an amount the portfolio is capable of losing before which all assets must be liquidated and shifted to a bond to ensure that it earns back the amount lost by the maturity date. The amount of acceptable loss will depend on market interest rate levels, and the amount of time remaining to product maturity. Suppose an investor begins with a portfolio of $100,000, and it is determined that, upon dropping to a $90,000 portfolio value, the portfolio is to be converted 100% into bonds. The acceptable loss level is known as the bond floor, in this example it is $10,000, and is amount beyond by which the CPPI portfolio should never fall in order to be able to ensure the notional guarantee at maturity.

The investor's portfolio in a CPPI product begins by being invested in a risky asset in the amount of (Multiplier) x (Bond Floor). A multiplier is calculated based on an assessment of an investor's risk profile for a maximum one-day loss. If it is decided that the most the risky asset is likely to lose is 25%, then the multiplier used is 1/25% = 4. In our example, CPPI will begin with (Multiplier) × (Bond floor) = 4 x $10,000 being invested in the risky asset (which equates to a 40% equity investment out of a $100,000 overall portfolio) and the remainder (60%) in the zero-coupon bond. CPPI, at the outset, allocates more of the investor's cash to a risky asset as compared to a structured product, or bond-and-call-option strategy, which allocates the residual cash left over after fees and the cost of a zero-coupon bond to a risky asset. , A structured product might be structured as 90% investment in a zero-coupon bond and 10% in a call option,

For our example, the investor will make an initial investment in the risky asset equal to the (Multiplier) × (Bond floor) and will invest the remainder in the zero-coupon bond. As the portfolio value changes over time, the investor will rebalance (timeframes for this will vary widely). If the equity value grows over time, more money can be allocated to the risky asset, while maintaining the same dollar portfolio floor. If the equity value falls over time, allocations to the risky asset will drop, to maintain the dollar portfolio floor.. The payoff of CPPI is somewhat similar to that of buying a call option, but does not involve the use of derivatives (however, note that trading in and out of the risky asset depending on performance bears resemblance to dynamic hedging strategies).

Are Structured Products "A Free Lunch?"

Structured products can go wrong in a number of ways:

1. The product may not be appropriate for the investor or suit their risk tolerance. There is some concern that these types of products are often mis-sold to retail investors who do not understand them and think they are getting a "free lunch."

2. The options may never pay off. In this case, while the end investor may get their principal back after five years, they will have actually lost money, as a dollar today is not worth the same as a

dollar in five years.

3. The fees may not be fair. Over time there has been increasing regulatory pressure for structured product issuers to disclose more of their fee information, but in many cases the high level of fees embedded in the structures can significantly reduce any legitimately anticipated returns should the option's ideal scenarios occur. Because of the complexity of the product combination (bond plus sometimes an unusual or illiquid option), and the largely retail investor base of the products, often customers are unable to appropriately evaluate and judge the fees charged to them.

4. Poor liquidity—an investor may be tied up for many years in these products, be unable to sell them at a fair price, and incur penalty fees for early termination.

5. A "principal guaranteed" bond might default and, as a result of this, in recent years issuers have moved to using the term "principal protected" rather than "principal guaranteed."

In the early stages of the financial crisis of 2007-2008, structured product issuance reached all-time highs. Many of the issuers and sellers of structured products were large investment banks. In many cases, the bond portion of the structured product was issued by these banks. In this case, the principal guarantee was based on the survival of the issuing investment bank.

For the vast majority of the time, this did not seem like a particularly risky aspect of structured products, but as the mid-2000s credit boom expanded, many of these institutions became highly-leveraged. When the housing/credit bubble burst in 2007-2008, a number of investment banks were unable to survive without government bail-outs and one major investment bank, Lehman Brothers, went bankrupt.

Ultimately, the purchasers of structured products are relying on the credit of the issuer. Prior to the collapse of the credit markets, many structured product purchasers had erroneously believed that the principal was guaranteed, in the way that government bonds are "guaranteed." This error was not always made explicitly clear to these (frequently retail and generally considered to be less sophisticated) investors. In the aftermath of the crisis, regulators attempted to rectify this by requiring structured product issuers to disclose very clearly the institution providing the principal guarantee in the documentation.

Lehman Brothers was the fourth largest investment bank in the United States when it collapsed in September 2008. It was a large issuer of structured products. Investors did not receive their principal guarantee because of the ultimate failure of the issuer. The bankruptcy left holders of these products waiting in line with other unsecured creditors for what was left of their money. Lehman estimated in 2011 that the average creditor would get about 18¢ on the dollar for $370 billion in claims payable by 2016.

6. Most structured products only have "long" asset exposure within the options portions of their structures. Because of the typically retail investor base, structures containing short bets are seen as too confusing, or unattractive, to market. While a long bias may make sense in markets that have upward drift such as equities, it makes less sense in structured products based on commodities or other underlyings.

7. Banks with bad credit ratings that might be unable to competitively issue principal-guaranteed structured products can buy principal insurance on these products from other higher rated banks or insurance companies. This led to contagion during the financial crisis of 2007-2008 where structured products from seemingly unrelated banks were causing large losses at other higher rated banks who had, shortly before this, accepted a very small premium to insure this principal-guarantee risk under their own names.

Transaction Costs

The fees embedded in structured products can be significant, sometimes 3-5% of the amounts invested, adding significant headwinds against investors to make money in these investments. Placement fees, structuring fees, and hedging costs all reduce the potential returns to investors. The products also typically do not have active secondary markets meaning that investors, once committed, often cannot readily liquidate their positions without incurring several percentage points of losses.

Over time, as the structured product market matures, fees should grind lower. This is particularly the case in more common or more commoditized products with more vanilla underlyings. The financial world is such a competitive space that a decline in fees is a natural progression over time. However, there remain exceptions for illiquid underlyings or for anything with a non-transparent forward or futures curve or options price.

Structured Products Today

Structured products issuance hasn't returned to its pre-financial crisis peak in part because of the difficulty of structuring attractive payouts to investors in a low interest rate environment. Low base rates leaves very little cash differential between the zero-coupon price at inception and the guaranteed bond payout at maturity, meaning that a limited quantity of options can be purchased to provide the conditional "upside" to investors.

Trading Strategy Structured Products

One of the evolutions in the world of structured products is the introduction of more hedge-fund like products coming into the structured product space. These structures are no longer a simple bond plus a call option, now structures can include a bond plus many options or active trading with a specified strategy of potentially multiple underlyings over the entire life of an investment's timeframe. Naturally it is much cheaper for the investment bank to offer a bond plus a call option in these structures from a hedging point of view. An active investment management strategy underlying a structured product would require full-time trading to offer the investors their promised returns profile, and likely only works financially for the bank if the structure is sold across a very large investor base.

Dynamic structured products are offered by many investment banks. An example would be a product that takes advantage of equity option premium. The issuers rely on research that has found that implied volatility is usually greater than realized volatility. A dynamic trading strategy underlying a structured product could seek to generate *alpha* (the excess return of an investment relative to the return of a benchmark index) by systematically selling options across diversified sectors and delta-hedging the portfolio to maturity to crystallize the difference between implied and realized equity volatility. An infinite variety of strategies underlying the structured product could be marketed as a dynamic structured product— essentially any active management or hedge-fund-style strategy.

Chapter 18 Questions

1. Why might an investor wish to purchase a structured note? Why might an issuer wish to sell one?

2. Are structured notes usually exchange listed products?

3. The great thing about a principal guaranteed product is that there is no way you can lose money. Discuss.

4. Why do structured products typically only offer long market exposures?

5. How does CPPI differ from the bond-plus-an-option style of structured product?

6. In CPPI, what is the multiplier, and how does it affect a structured product?

7. Give two examples of where structured products can go wrong.

8. What are dynamic structured products? Why might issuers be happy to issue them when they require more effort to maintain than a vanilla structured product?

Chapter 19

FINANCIAL DERIVATIVES AND CORPORATE FINANCE

Options theory has provided insights into many areas of finance, including *Corporate Finance,* or the analysis and valuation of stocks and bonds. Robert Merton proposed in 1974 that the capital structure of a firm can be analyzed using *contingent claims theory.* Contingent claim refers to a payoff that is dependent on the value of another underlying asset -- the example that Merton was specifically referring to is the value of equity in a company being viewed as contingent on the value and of the company's debt. Should a company be close to bankruptcy, the value of the equity of the firm will be at or very close to zero, because equity has only a residual claim on a company's value after debt obligations have been met.

For example, consider at a simple form of company, one with equity holders along with a single bond outstanding. For simplification purposes we will assume this is a discount bond, with no coupons to pay prior to its maturity. It is possible to show that the equity value of a firm is similar to a call option on the entire value of the firm with a strike price equivalent to the debt outstanding to bondholders.

Equally, the bond can be analyzed to reveal *optionality* or option-like behavior. The corporate bond can be viewed as a riskless bond plus a short put position on the value of the firm.

In many cases, companies have more complex corporate structures—multiple classes of equity, with different voting and dividend rights, along with multiple bond issuances and bank loans. However, a pared down version of the potentially complex mix of debt and equities held relating to a firm's value can illustrate the optionality embedded in corporate stakeholdings.

The Merton Model

In corporate finance, the value of a firm is equal to the present value of the firm's expected future cash flows. The firm value must also be equal to the total value of its outstanding equities and debt instruments.

$$V = E + D$$

Where:

V = the firm's value

E = the firm's total equity value

D = the firm's total debt value

The bond valuation in this example, seeing as it is a pure discount bond with no coupons to be paid, only principal or face value (FV) to be repaid at maturity, time T, is worth:

$$D = e^{(-rT)}FV$$

Here, the discount rate (r) is a risky discount rate, reflecting the appropriate riskiness of the bond in question.

At maturity, the firm will either repay the face value of the bond, or it will default. If the firm defaults, the bondholders will take over the assets of the firm at that point in time. They will aim to recoup as much of their investment as possible.

If the firm is worth more than the face value of its debt at maturity, the company will repay the debt, and the firm will then be entirely equity-financed, or equity held. Therefore, at the maturity of the bond, the equity holders hold a position worth either 0 (in the case of bond default) or V − FV. Therefore, the firm's equity valuation is similar to a European call option, with a payoff of

$$E_T = \max(0,[V_T - FV])$$

This is equivalent to a call option with a strike of the face value of the debt outstanding, where the underlying asset is the value of the firm itself.

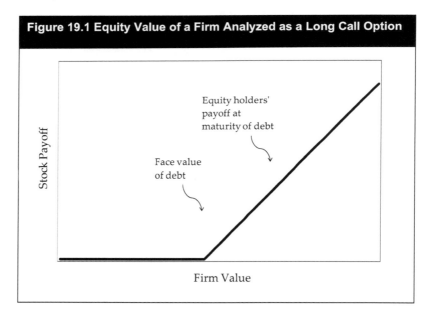

Figure 19.1 Equity Value of a Firm Analyzed as a Long Call Option

Figure 19.1 shows the payoff profile of the equity holders of the firm, at maturity of the debt. If the firm valuation is below the strike price, the face value of the debt, the equity holders receive nothing. Any value in excess of the debt's face value is held on to by the equity holders in the non-default case.

We therefore know that the minimum value of E, the equity holders' stake, is the current firm value less the present value of the debt, or

$$E_0 >= V_0 - FVe^{-rT}$$

An interesting insight arises here, where we note that for all long options holders, the option's value increases as volatility increases. If the underlying firm decides to take on an increasingly risky corporate strategy, this will make the call option more valuable (i.e., will increase the value of E to all equity holders).

In most corporate settings, good corporate governance entails management of the firm to enhance shareholder value as its primary priority. But here we note that this option-like payoff means that equity holders have a direct incentive to increase the riskiness of the underlying firm. If the higher risk corporate strategies are successful, then the equity holders keep this upside. If the increased risk profile fails, the losses to equity holders are limited to their original investments, through the limited liability nature of equity investments. Stock holders stand to gain considerably from higher risk management practices, but can only suffer limited losses.

It should be noted that because the value of the firm is simply the sum of the equity holders' stake plus the bondholders' stake, any excess value that equity holders extract from the firm must be at the expense of the only other stakeholder.

This is intuitive to experienced bond investors, and bond ratings agencies, since the greater the risks an underlying firm is taking, the greater likelihood of firm bankruptcy or debt default. As such, many debt instruments include covenants that attempt to restrict company management from undertaking excessively risky projects, or increasing their overall indebtedness to an extent that will undermine bondholders' value.

In our simplified corporate example, the equity holders have promised to repay the debt holders a maximum amount. The best the debt holders can do is be repaid in full at maturity, at face value.

The firm's management will only repay them if the firm value exceeds the debt's face value. Otherwise, they will hand the firm over to the debt holders. Thus, at maturity of the debt, the payoff to debt holders is as follows:

$$D_T = min(V_T, FV)$$

Since

$$V = D + E$$

then

$$D = V - E$$

or

$$D = V - max(0, V_T - FV)$$

Another way of viewing this is that the debt holders will at most receive face value (FV) at all upside scenarios for the total value of the firm at bond maturity. In all other cases, they will receive the firm value, with the debt holders' payout declining in a linear fashion, along with any declines in the total firm's value. This payoff can be shown as follows:

$$D = FV - max(0, FV - V_T)$$

This is precisely the payoff of a short put option, with a strike of FV, plus a riskless bond with the same face value. This can be viewed in two ways, either as ownership of the firm plus a short call option on the firm with a strike price at the face value of the bond; or, as a risk-free bond paying face value, and a short put option with a strike price of the face value of the bond. This is consistent with put-call parity which shows that the relationship between equity, puts, calls, and a risk-free bond must hold (for European options with the same strikes and maturity) of:

$$S - c = K(e^{-rT}) - p$$

In our example, we are looking at the entire value of the firm, V, as the underlying, instead of S as the underlying. Here we have:

$$V - c = FV(e^{-rT}) - p$$

Note that r here as a discount rate is riskless, as the riskiness of the bond repayment is incorporated in the short put position. Figure 19.2 illustrates corporate debt's option-like payoff profile.

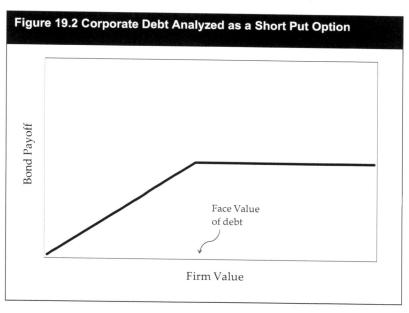

Figure 19.2 Corporate Debt Analyzed as a Short Put Option

In a more realistic, or complex firm structure, debt with various levels of seniority can be viewed as having different strike prices in the option-like valuation of the firm equity.

Option Embedded Bonds

Many bonds are *callable*, meaning that the bond issuers have the right to call or redeem the bond after paying a specified fee. Often there are provisions that the bond may not be called within the first several years of issuance. After this, they can be called if it is beneficial to the underlying issuing company. This should happen anytime the coupon rate on the bond exceeds the current rate that the company is able to borrow at in the market. Clearly, to bondholders, a *callable bond* is less valuable than a noncallable bond. As soon as an interest rate becomes very attractive to the coupon recipient, versus what they would now be able to achieve investing in a company of similar risk, the bond will be "called away" from them. The bondholder, at the time they invest in a callable bond, is therefore buying a standard bond plus selling a call option on the bond to the issuing company.

In line with earlier discussions of options theory, the short call option's value will vary with the time remaining to maturity, market interest rates, noncallable bond values, and the volatility of the bonds in question.

Figure 19.3 illustrates the pricing relationship between callable and noncallable bonds. For interest rates below which the bond can be called, the callable bond's value is capped at the call price.

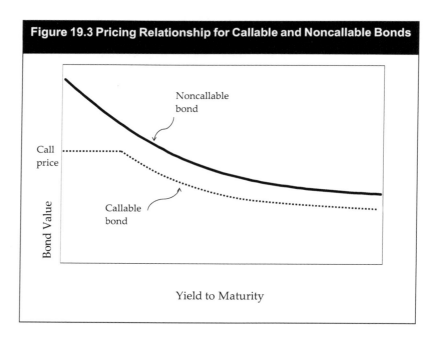

Figure 19.3 Pricing Relationship for Callable and Noncallable Bonds

Convertible Bonds

Many corporate bonds can be converted into equity positions when certain conditions are met. The bondholder chooses when and if to exercise this option to convert into an equity holding. This type of bond is valued as a straight bond plus a warrant. Issuers are able to pay lower interest rates compared to standard bond rates in similar market conditions at the time of issuance of *convertible bonds*. This is attractive for firms who are hoping to keep their coupon payments lower. This is attractive for investors who perceive upside in the equity valuation of the firm, and are willing to forgo some value in the form of receiving lower bond coupons in order to receive potential value in the form of the embedded warrant.

Warrants

Warrants are another form of corporate security with embedded optionality. Warrants are issued by the company itself and raise capital for the firm upon issuance. This is in contrast to call options which are created by exchanges, and generate no capital for underlying firms. Warrants are similar to call options on stocks in that the owners can exchange them, at the warrant-owner's discretion, for shares in the company, and pay a pre-set price for the shares, much like the strike in a call option contract. Warrants are sometimes tacked onto bond issuances to entice investors to invest in a company's bonds. Once warrants are exercised, they are dilutive to the firm's capital structure since new shares must be issued by the company. Warrants are in most ways extremely similar to call options, with the exception of the dilution to shares outstanding to the firm. As such, warrants are worth:

$$w = \frac{c}{(1 + \frac{new\ shares\ created}{prior\ shares\ outstanding})}$$

Capital Structure Arbitrage

Capital structure arbitrage is one of the newer hedge fund trading strategies. It became quite a popular trade in the 1990s, and increased in size when the CDS market expanded through the 2000s. It is built around the ideas that Robert Merton first proposed in 1974. If the capital structure of a firm can be analyzed using contingent claims theory, debt holders can be regarded as having sold a put option on the market value of the firm; while equity holders' investment in the firm's value, after its debt obligations, resembles a call option. Then options pricing theory can be used to analyze the relationship between the value of a firm's debt and its equity.

Structural models assume that default occurs when the market value of the firm falls below a clearly defined threshold, determined by the size of the firm's debt obligations. If the market value of the firm can be modeled as a stochastic process, it is then possible to calculate an estimated default probability for the firm.

While there are numerous structural models, they have similar inputs. The key inputs are:

1. The capital structure of the firm
2. The market value of the firm
3. The volatility of the firm's market value

Structural models all imply that the credit risk of a firm rises as its stock price falls, but the relationship is nonlinear and is most noticeable when the stock price is quite low.

When searching for relative value opportunities, the capital structure arbitrageur uses a structural model to gauge the expensiveness and cheapness of the credit spread. Using the market value of equity, a volatility measure for the firm, and the liability structure of the company, they compare the spread implied from the model with the market spread. When the market spread is substantially different to the theoretical spread implied in the traders' models, they trade the credit against equity. If the market and equity-implied spread from the model then converge, a profit is made. The model helps identify credits that are either trading "cheaply" against equities or credits trading "expensively" versus their associated equity.

A Reminder on Arbitrage

Arbitrage is the simultaneous purchase and sale of an equivalent asset in two venues in order to profit from a difference in the price. True arbitrage should be riskless, based on equivalent assets and the profits should be instantaneous. Many hedge fund strategies have the term arbitrage in their titles but involve some kind of risk, time delay, and non-equivalent assets.

Why Might an Opportunity Exist in Capital Structure Arbitrage?

Fixed income and equity securities traditionally have different investor bases. This fact could possibly give rise to "relative mispricings" of the two assets. If a firm existed where the bonds were pricing in a distressed outlook for the company and, at the same time, the equity of the company was trading as though the company is healthy and on track to repay debt obligations, pay dividends, and achieve capital gains for equity-holders, a profitable trading opportunity might exist. In this case an investor might choose to buy the "cheap" bonds and sell the "expensive" equity and hope the market begins to price the two securities more rationally. Sizing the two relative positions is of great importance in this trade. Equity and debt do not have clear, consistent betas to each other.

The existence of a variety of instruments available for trading gives rise to numerous ways to express views in the capital arbitrage space, and numerous instruments to evaluate "cheapness" and "expensiveness." Traders can use equities, bonds, options, credit default swaps, and convertible bonds to take long/short capital structure arbitrage positions.

Capital Structure Arbitrage Returns

Capital structure arbitrage has been found to be quite risky at the level of individual trades. As a relatively new hedge fund strategy, it is difficult to analyze long-term returns. The strategy is typically most effective when companies are at or near a distress situation. The models are extremely sensitive to model assumptions. Within this strategy the "hedged" positions between a firm's equity and bond instruments may be ineffective in practice, and the two markets may continue to diverge, resulting in losses and early liquidations.

Chapter 19 Questions

1. Describe how the equity value of a firm is like a call option.

2. Draw a diagram of the payoff to debt holders of a firm that has one bond outstanding, with no remaining coupons (only principal remaining) at maturity. The only stakeholders in the firm are the bond's holders and common equity shareholders.

3. Explain with reference to the Merton Model (1974) how a company's capital structure can be viewed as options?

4. Why might a bond investor be incentivized to restrict the volatility of a business, while the equity investor in the same firm might be incentivized to pursue more volatile business lines?

5. What is capital structure arbitrage? Within what type of company might this strategy be most effective and why?

6. Why are convertible bonds referred to as hybrid securities?

7. Is capital structure arbitrage a true arbitrage? Explain.

8. Should a callable bond be priced higher or lower than an otherwise identical noncallable bond? Explain.

9. Explain how corporate debt can be viewed as a short put option.

Chapter 20

REAL OPTIONS

The *Real Options* valuation approach is an extension of financial options theory that we have covered so far, to options on real (non-financial) assets. Real options are not actual derivative instruments, they are real decisions that a business manager may have to make. Decisions such as whether to invest in a new project, whether to downsize, or whether to expand internationally. Real options analysis applies option valuation techniques to analyzing these types of decisions. For example, the opportunity to invest in a new retail outlet, or alternatively to shut down a division, is a real call or real put option, respectively. Other examples of real options may be opportunities for R&D, M&A, and licensing.

Traditional Methods of Project Analysis

There are three common tools used by managers to value investment opportunities: (1) payback rules, (2) accounting rates of return, and (3) net present value.

Payback rules ask how many periods management must wait before cumulative cash flows from a project exceed the cost of the investment.

Accounting rate of return is the ratio of the average forecast profits over the project's lifetime (after depreciation and taxes) to the average book value of the investment.

Net Present Value (NPV) is the difference between the present value of projected cash inflows and the present value of projected cash outflows of a project. Real options analysis is an approach that can be added to this toolkit.

Payback rules, while simple to calculate, just set a hurdle in terms of return of capital initially invested, but ignore subsequent cash flows, whether positive or negative. The accounting rate of return approach and the NPV approach both work well if you are projecting future cash flows from a historical context, and you are fairly certain of future expectations. These approaches don't do as well when your estimate of future cash flows is based on myriad assumptions about what the future may hold. In such cases, the odds of accurately projecting future cash flows are low.

Embedded Options

The types of options that may be embedded in a project are and that a financial practitioner or businessperson might seek to value include:

- The option to delay making an investment
- The option to adjust production schedules as prices change
- The option to expand the scope or scale of a project at later stages in the process, based upon favorable outcomes in early stages
- The option to abandon an investment if the outcomes are unfavorable at early stages

Options are contingent decisions, they give an investor the opportunity to make a decision after they have seen how events unfold. Option payoffs are usually nonlinear. The real options approach values the ability to invest now and make follow-up decisions later based upon the success of a project. Certain kinds of business decisions have embedded optionality -- taking certain courses of action can open up future potential angles, whereas not pursuing some projects can close down future potential business choices. Pharmaceutical R&D for example can have a lot of optionality embedded in it. Businesses like mining or oil exploration are good examples, too, where the main uncertainty is the commodity price.

Real Options Valuation

In valuing real options, there has to be a clearly defined underlying asset whose value changes over time in unpredictable ways. The payoffs on this asset (the real option) have to be contingent on a specified event occurring within a finite period.

Questions you must ask yourself before deciding to use the real options approach are: Is there clearly an option embedded in this asset or decision? Can I specify the contingency under which I will get a payoff? Is the cost of exercising the option known and clear?

Discounted cash flow (DCF) analysis involves coming up with an accurate estimate of the project's cash flows and then discounting them at a high rate to reflect the risks of achieving the projected returns. All of the risks of uncertainty are captured in the valuation, but the possibility that actual cash flows may be much higher than forecast are not. This bias can lead managers to reject promising, but uncertain, projects. The possibility that the project may deliver on the high end of potential forecasts is the primary driver of option value. DCF valuation can be used to create a base estimate of value with real options analysis being used to value the impact of large potential upside combined with the ability to abandon an unsuccessful project before the full investment has been made.

Real options analysis can be useful for valuing new businesses where the metrics typically used to value established stable businesses might not be applicable. A new business may have negative earnings as it spends money in order to grow. A model of the business's growth and eventual future cash-flows may be built with a number of variables such as sales growth, staffing costs, profit margins, emergence of competitors, and so on. A Monte Carlo analysis can then generate a variety of different paths that cash flows could follow, and present value them such that a reasonable valuation for the company is arrived at.

Not all Projects Have Optionality

- When there are no options embedded in the project
- When there is little uncertainty
- When the consequences of uncertainty can be ignored

Most real-world projects contain some optionality, whether they are options to delay investment, to expand a project, or to abandon a project that is not working out. The relative amounts that real-option and DCF valuations contribute to a project's total value vary with the project's uncertainty.

Real Options Inputs

While the real options approach avoids the need to calculate a discount rate as is used in DCF analysis, it does require market prices for a variety of inputs into the pricing formula. The inputs required for modeling a real option correspond to those required for a financial option valuation. The underlying is the project in question. The spot price is usually the project's net present value (NPV). Volatility is usually derived from the volatility of a substitute, such as the listed stock of a company that is in the business in question, or the volatility of a similar project that the company already invests in. If you are using a listed security to model volatility, if options exist on this security you can use its implied volatility.

The strike price is usually any non-recoverable investment outlays. The expiration is the time during which management may decide to act, or not act. Given the flexibility related to timing as described, caution must be applied here. The options are usually modeled as American options as early exercise is possible.

Example

Fintechia, a financial technology company based in Silicon Valley, is experiencing a lot of growth. They have two years left on their current office space lease, but anticipate that if they continue to grow, they will need to secure a much larger space. The current price per square foot of office buildings in Mountain View, California, is $100 with a five-year lease. The size they anticipate they may need, in a good economic scenario, is 10,000 square feet, which equates to annual rent of $1,000,000.

The CEO is concerned that if they wait until their current lease expires to strike a new lease, the price per square foot could go up. However, if the business does not grow as anticipated, they fear they cannot cover the costs of a larger office space with a five year commitment. How much would Fintechia be willing to pay to secure the right but not the obligation to lease $100 per square foot office space for a five year timeframe, starting in two years? Assume that the entire five years of rent would be paid in advance on the move in date. A listed Real Estate Investment Trust (REIT), that operates mostly in the same geographical area, which has no outstanding debt, has options trading on it with an implied volatility of 15%. The risk-free rate is 5%.

The underlying, in terms of real options pricing, is the present value of the entire rental cost, which in this case is approximately $4.12 million. The strike of the option is the full rental cost of $5 million, given that this is what the company would have to pay, in two years, should they wish to take on the five-year lease at that point. Suppose that Fintechia could purchase this option now, the right but not the obligation to rent this space for 5 years, at $100 per square foot annually starting in two years' time, and that the option can be exercised in exactly two years. Using the Black-Scholes formula, an option to enter into this lease in two years' time is valued at $199,017.

Flaws in the Real Options Methodology

Here are criticisms of the real options approach:

1. Real options can overestimate the value of uncertain projects, encouraging over-ambitious managers to gamble with shareholders' money.
2. Real options analysis requires a lot of simplifying assumptions which may not capture the big picture of a new project.
3. It can be hard to find good proxies for the input variables the model requires. There are often no numbers available to derive the option value of an innovative project.
4. The more variables in a project being analyzed using the real options framework, the higher the project valuation will be. This can lead to an impractical result, valuing a project with relatively unpredictable revenues but predictable costs more highly than a project with predictable revenues and with predictable costs, (building in an additional cost for an unknown even if that cost might go down)
5. The time period used in the calculation can be extremely problematic. With a financial option, the more time there is to expiration, the more valuable the option. This makes perfect sense with financial options but the underlying logic does not hold in the case of project evaluation where delaying a product launch should not be expected to add value to a project. In such a scenario, you end up waiting longer for cash flows and could even end up being beaten to the market by competitors.
6. Like every other model, real options analysis suffers from the "garbage in, garbage out" problem.

Conclusion

Realistically, with highly uncertain projects, any valuation method, no matter how sophisticated, will often be wrong. Any time spent worrying about the exact option value of a project is time wasted. All any valuation method can be expected to do is establish relative values within a group of opportunities, giving managers a means of ranking investment opportunities, so that they can select the most promising.

Managers have a variety of tools to evaluate uncertain projects. The real options approach is a useful tool, but it does not have to replace all other approaches, and of course should not be followed blindly. Combining this approach with other more traditional approaches can enable senior managers to, in the long run, select better projects than their competitors while keeping risk under control.

Chapter 20 Questions

1. Explain the difference between the NPV approach and the real options approach to valuing a project. What are the advantages and disadvantages of each approach?

2. How are payback rules used in project evaluation? What are the advantages and disadvantages of this approach?

3. How are the market prices of the various option pricing inputs typically gathered in order to evaluate an innovative project using real options?

4. In a scenario where a project is being evaluated using the real options approach, but we are unsure of the correct volatility figure to use, what could we do in order to nonetheless do some useful analysis?

5. Explain how the Monte Carlo approach could be used to value a new business which is not cash flow positive?

6. In using the Monte Carlo approach to value a new business which is not cash flow positive, how would we deal with the potential for bankruptcy?

7. Explain how the time period used in real options analysis for project evaluation can be problematic?

8. What inputs might cause the real options value of a potential project to be significantly higher than the same project evaluated using traditional valuation approaches? Is this ever problematic?

9. If five managers independently value a project using a variety of tools, and each manager comes back with entirely different valuations, is there any point to having done this analysis? Explain.

10. Explain three criticisms of the real options approach.

Subject Index

Made in the USA
Las Vegas, NV
08 November 2023

80476210R00171